CAMBRIDGE
Global English

Coursebook

7

Chris Barker and Libby Mitchell

CAMBRIDGE
UNIVERSITY PRESS

University Printing House, Cambridge CB2 8BS, United Kingdom

Cambridge University Press is part of the University of Cambridge.

It furthers the University's mission by disseminating knowledge in the pursuit of education, learning and research at the highest international levels of excellence.

Information on this title: education.cambridge.org

First published 2014
5th printing 2015

Printed in the United Kingdom by Latimer Trend

A catalogue record for this publication is available from the British Library

ISBN 978-1-107-67807-1 Learner's Book with Audio CD

Welcome to Cambridge Global English Stage 7

Cambridge Global English is an eight-stage course for learners of English as a Second Language (ESL). The eight stages range from the beginning of primary (Stages 1-6) to the end of the first two years of junior secondary (Stages 7–8). It is ideal for all international ESL learners, and particularly for those following the Cambridge Primary/Secondary English as a Second Language Curriculum Framework, as it has been written to adhere to this framework. It presents realistic listening, speaking, reading and writing tasks, as well as end-of-unit projects similar to those students might encounter in the context of a first-language school. The course is organised into eighteen thematic units of study based on the Cambridge International English Scheme of Work for Stage 7. After every other unit, there is a literature spread, featuring authentic prose, poetry, plays and songs from a variety of sources.

Cambridge Global English materials are aligned with the Common European Framework of Reference. The materials reflect the following principles:

- *An international focus.* Specifically developed for young learners throughout the world, the topics and situations in *Cambridge Global English* have been selected to reflect this diversity and encourage learning about each other's lives through the medium of English.

- *A cross-curricular, language-rich approach to learning.* *Cambridge Global English* engages learners actively and creatively. At the same time as participating in a range of curriculum-based activities, they practise English language and literacy and develop critical thinking skills.

- *English for educational success.* To meet the challenges of the future, learners will need to develop facility with both conversational and more formal English. From the earliest stage, *Cambridge Global English* addresses both these competencies. Emphasis is placed on developing the listening, speaking, reading and writing skills learners will need to be successful in using English-language classroom materials.

In addition to this Coursebook, *Cambridge Global English Workbook 7* provides supplementary support and practice. Comprehensive support for teachers is available in *Cambridge Global English Teacher's Resource 7*.

We hope that learners and teachers enjoy using *Cambridge Global English Stage 7* as much as we have enjoyed writing it.

Chris Barker and Libby Mitchell

Contents

	Reading/Topic	Listening/Speaking	Use of English	Vocabulary	Writing
Unit 1 **Meeting and greeting**	Customs of meeting and greeting Special greetings and social expressions A quiz on social customs and politeness Gift-giving and famous gifts in history	**Listening** Responding to social scenarios with an appropriate expression Customs associated with gift-giving in India **Speaking** Greet people formally and informally Talk about ways of greeting Make up and roleplay dialogues using special greetings and social expressions Talk about gift-giving	Modals: *should, can, could, may*	Greetings and ways of greeting (*nod your head, shake hands*) Social expressions (*Congratulations!, Have a nice weekend.*)	A paragraph about meeting and greeting people in your culture
Project	Write a guide to social customs in your country				
Unit 2 **Personal identity**	Life at school First impressions: the first few weeks at secondary school A scientific approach to family history	**Listening** A conversation between two students doing a class survey **Speaking** Ask and answer questions in a class survey Ask and answer questions about family members	Present perfect for situations continuing up to now Apostrophes *'s* and *s'*	Family	A description of your family A profile of the oldest person in your family
Project Fiction Review	Write a report about your impressions of school so far this term *Hullabaloo in the Guava Orchard* by Kiran Desai Review of Units 1–2				
Unit 3 **Clothing and accessories**	Clothes and fashion The clothes and accessories of the ancient Egyptians An advert for an accessory	**Listening** Clothes from around the world Adverts for accessories **Speaking** Give your views on clothes and fashion Give your views on accessories Talk about clothes from around the world	Phrasal verbs (*shop for, try on*) Present passive, including modals with passive (*it can be worn with …*)	Clothes and parts of clothes (*sleeve, button*) Materials (*cotton, gold*)	A paragraph about your attitudes to clothes and fashion A paragraph about a traditional item of clothing
Project	Prepare and give a presentation of a product				
Unit 4 **Outdoor pursuits**	Outdoor sports and activities in New Zealand An article in a travel magazine Messages and other documents relating to a holiday Activity holidays School trips	**Listening** A conversation about an adventure holiday Information about a school trip **Speaking** Describe sports and outdoor pursuits Ask and answer about experiences (*Have you ever … ?*) Talk about what you'll be doing at a certain time	Present perfect with *ever* Expressing the future *-ing* forms as subjects, objects and after a preposition	Outdoor pursuits Outdoor survival skills	Sentences about what you like doing and are good at
Project Poetry and song Review	Planning a school trip *Postcard from School Camp* by Richard Caley, *Forty Years on an Iceberg* Review of Units 3–4				
Unit 5 **Transport systems**	An article about transport systems around the world A brief history of public transport Road signs and road safety	**Listening** An account of the first hot-air balloon flights A discussion about road safety **Speaking** Describe types of transport Talk about the advantages of different kinds of transport	Past simple passive (with *by*) *wish (that)* + past simple	Types of transport and words related to transport (*passenger, fare*) Traditional and historic means of transport (*raft, locomotive*) Traffic signs	An account of the first hot-air balloon flights A 'wish list' for your school
Project	Preparing and presenting a plan for improving travel to and from school				

	Reading/Topic	Listening/Speaking	Use of English	Vocabulary	Writing
Unit 6 **Using maps**	Street maps and transport maps Map reading A newspaper report of a mountain rescue	**Listening** A phone conversation about finding your way in a city A phone conversation about travelling on the subway/metro A radio news report of a mountain rescue **Speaking** Role play a conversation about finding your way and travelling in a city	Prepositions to do with travel (*on the subway, get on/off*) Comparative adjectives using *much ... than* and *(not) as ... as* Past continuous, including passive form	Places and buildings in a town or city Symbols and places on a map	Write down the details of a phone conversation
Project **Fiction** **Review**	Write a newspaper article about a rescue operation *The Dream* from *One Thousand and One Nights* Review of Units 5–6				
Unit 7 **Health, food and exercise**	A balanced diet An information leaflet on healthy eating A leaflet on what the brain needs to work well A magazine article about the diet and training of Kenyan long-distance runners	**Listening** A nutritionist answering questions about diet and health **Speaking** Talking about a balanced diet Ask and answer about diet, exercise and routine	Quantifiers with countable and uncountable nouns (*a few, a little*) Adjectives and adverbs Comparatives of adverbs Position of adverbs of frequency	Food The science of food (*protein, carbohydrates*) Scientific words related to diet and healthy living (*oxygen, dehydration*)	Write questions about routine, food and exercise
Project	Plan a menu				
Unit 8 **All living things**	Animal groups Descriptions of the characteristics of animals from different groups Family resemblances Inherited characteristics A magazine article and a fact file about the world of the polar bear and habitat shift	**Listening** Listen to and follow information about animals **Speaking** Answer questions about animals Talk about who you look like and take after in your family Talk about interests, abilities and inherited characteristics	*so am I, so do I* Relative clauses with *which* as a subject pronoun	Characteristics of different types of animal Physical characteristics (*curly hair*)	Questions about animals
Project **Fiction** **Review**	Write a fact file about bears in the wild *War Horse* by Michael Morpurgo Review of Units 7–8				
Unit 9 **World records**	An illustrated history of the ancient Olympics Spectators' comments on the Paralympics A profile of an athlete A world records quiz	**Listening** A profile of a Paralympic athlete **Speaking** Talk about the similarities and differences between the ancient Olympics and the modern Olympics Ask and answer questions about an athlete Take part in a world records quiz	Past perfect Pronouns *everyone, anyone, no one, everything, anything, nothing* Comparatives and superlatives of adverbs	Words relating to the Olympic Games	Write an account giving your impressions of a sporting event
Project	Write a biography of an athlete				
Unit 10 **Parts and percentages**	The language of Maths A numbers quiz The golden ratio and how it works A class survey	**Listening** Follow instructions in number games **Speaking** Solve maths puzzles Discuss the golden ratio Talk about places and buildings (*It's a lake / a famous building in ...*) Do a class survey and discuss the results	Place names and buildings with and without *the* Part and percentages: expressions of quantity followed by *of*	Mathematical words (*add, subtract*) Geometric shapes (*pyramid, rectangle*)	Write examples of places, buildings and geographical features Rewrite parts and percentages in words
Project **Fiction** **Review**	Design and carry out a survey *To Give* by Vimal Shinagadia Review of Units 9–10				

	Reading/Topic	Listening/Speaking	Use of English	Vocabulary	Writing
Unit 11 **We're going on holiday!**	Types of holiday Holiday plans and experiences Text messages to do with travel Airports School exchanges	**Listening** Holiday plans **Speaking** Talk about holidays Report what someone said in a text message Ask and answer questions about holidays. Report your conversation.	Compound nouns (*water sports, day trip*) Verbs followed by the *-ing* form Reported speech: statements and questions	Types of holiday and holiday accommodation Sports facilities and holiday activities Features of the landscape Airport signs	Write text messages as if at an airport Write questions about holidays Write a postcard from a holiday destination
Project	Plan a special holiday treat for a friend or for a member of your family				
Unit 12 **Climate and the environment**	The weather Global warming and extreme weather A magazine article about a zero-carbon city	**Listening** A weather forecast A science programme explaining thunder and lightning **Speaking** Give a weather forecast Talk about the causes of thunder and lightning Give your views on cities of the future	Present simple active and passive in scientific writing	The weather Collocations to do with the weather (*heavy rain, strong winds*) Extreme weather Scientific and technical words to do with the environment and renewable energy (*natural resources, solar energy*)	Write a weather forecast for a particular area
Project **Fiction** **Review**	Find out about an eco house and give a presentation *Rain Falls Down* by Margot Henderson; *Your Dresses* by Carol Ann Duffy Review of Units 11–12				
Unit 13 **In and out of school**	Education and learning styles A website forum about talking in class An excerpt from a school prospectus International penpals A letter from a penpal	**Listening** A parent talking to a headteacher about aspects of a school **Speaking** Give your views on talking in class Discuss what helps you to learn Compare your school with a free school Talk about what you have in common with a penpal	Prepositions followed by the *-ing* form (*by comparing, instead of interrupting*) Verbs followed by the infinitive with *to*	Aspects of school: classroom interaction, timetable, subjects, facilities, after-school activities	A paragraph about how you learn best
Project	Write a letter to a penpal				
Unit 14 **Local community**	Shops and services Town and country You and your community A multiple-choice test about how responsible you are	**Listening** Young people talking about what they do to help in their community **Speaking** Talk about shops and services Talk about whether you'd like to live in the town or the country Compare your answers to a multiple-choice test	*to have something done* Second conditional (*if* clauses to describe imaginary situations)	Shops and services Adjectives to describe town and country (*quiet, crowded; traffic, pollution*)	A paragraph about where you would like to live in the future
Project **Poetry** **Review**	Prepare and give a presentation about how to improve your local area *In Daylight Strange* by Alan Brownjohn Review Units 13–14				

	Reading/Topic	Listening/Speaking	Use of English	Vocabulary	Writing
Unit 15 **Settling America**	The first Americans The pioneer families Stories from the American West *Rachel's Journal*, an American girl's diary from 1850	**Listening** A story from the wagon train **Speaking** Talk about the important things in life	Abstract nouns (*independence, hope*) Compound nouns (*wagon train, log cabin*) Expressing the past (revision of present perfect, past simple and past continuous)	Words connected with the settling of America (*settlers, pioneers*)	Write questions about pioneer families and their journey west across America
Project	Write a diary entry as if from a wagon train in the 1850s				
Unit 16 **The Silk Road**	The Silk Road A traditional story from Uzbekistan	**Listening** A description of the journey along the Silk Road The conclusion of the story *A Rainbow in Silk* **Speaking** Describe the journey along the Silk Road Talk about goods that are imported and exported Ask and answer questions about a story Compare two versions of a story	Participles used as adjectives (*bored, boring*) *so* and *such* to add emphasis	Positive and negative adjectives and adverbs (*beautiful, disappointed, brightly, anxiously*)	Complete a summary of a story
Project **Poetry** **Review**	Creative writing: Write the conclusion to a story *Akbar and Birbal*, traditional stories Review of Units 15–16				
Unit 17 **Festivals around the world**	Festivals New Year celebrations An account of three festivals: Diwali, Eid al-Fitr, Maslenitsa April Fools' Day	**Listening** A description of New Year traditions and celebrations Accounts of fun days (April Fools' Days) around the world **Speaking** Ask and answer questions about Chinese New Year Talk about three festivals Talk about fun days and festivals	Prepositional phrases (*in January, at midnight*) Compound adjectives (*brightly-coloured*)	Words connected with celebrations (*festivities, fireworks*)	An account of how you and your family celebrate New Year An account of a festival in your country A newspaper story to appear on April Fools' Day
Project	Create an information poster about a festival				
Unit 18 **Using English**	The theatre Performing in a play The story of *Aladdin*	**Listening** The conclusion of the story of *Aladdin* **Speaking** Talk about being in a play Give an opinion of a story	*like* and *as* to say that things are similar Reported speech: commands	The theatre (*actor, stage*) Words from the story of *Aladdin* (*sorcerer, genie*)	Write an account of a play you've been in or about the role you would like to have in a play
Project **Review**	Write and perform a play, based on the story of *Aladdin* Review of Units 17–18				

1 Meeting and greeting

- **Topics** Customs of meeting and greeting; special greetings and social expressions (*Have a good weekend*); gift-giving and famous gifts in history
- **Use of English** Modals: *should, can, could, may*

How do you say hello?

- Do you know any words for hello and goodbye in other languages?

Speaking

1 Work with a partner. Which of the following phrases are for friends and family? Which would you use with your teachers?

Hello	Good morning	Hi
How are you?	All right?	See you
How's it going?	Goodbye	Bye
Good afternoon	How are things?	

Reading and listening 🔲2

2 Read about how people greet each other and guess which country they come from. Then listen and check.

Argentina	Thailand	Singapore	India

Did you know?

In the UK, when someone asks, 'How are you?' people often reply, 'I'm fine, thanks', or 'I'm very well, thank you'. In other words, people always pretend to be OK even if they're not. You can only break this rule with a really good friend. Is this true in your culture?

1 I'm from _____ . When we meet someone for the first time, we usually nod our heads and smile. In formal situations, we shake hands.

2 In _____ , women give one kiss on the cheek when they greet friends and family. In formal situations, people shake hands.

3 In _____ , close friends and family members hug when they meet, but they do not kiss. You only kiss babies and very young children.

4 In _____ , we don't hug or kiss each other when we meet. We greet friends and colleagues with 'wai'. Wai is a gesture. You put your hands together and bow your head. The tips of your thumbs should touch your chin for a friend and your nose for someone older than you. However, today younger people usually wave and even hug.

Vocabulary

3 Complete these collocations. They are all in the text.

1 to nod your *head*
2 to s_____ hands with someone
3 to put your _____ together
4 to bow your _____
5 to give someone a _____ on the cheek

4 Match the words and phrases from the text with their meanings.

1 formal
2 cheek
3 to hug
4 colleagues
5 gesture
6 tip
7 to wave

a people you work with
b a movement of the hand, arms or head to express something
c the side of your face
d to move your hand when saying hello or goodbye
e following social customs and accepted ways of behaving
f to put your arms round someone
g the narrow or pointed end of something

Speaking

5 Work with a partner. Answer these questions about meeting and greeting in your culture.

1 What do you do when you meet someone of your own age for the first time?
2 What do you do when you meet an adult for the first time?
3 How do you greet family members and close friends?

Writing

6 Use your answers to the questions in Exercise 5 to write a paragraph about meeting and greeting in your culture.

When we meet someone of our own age for the first time, we _____

Speaking

7 Look at these pictures of people greeting each other. Describe them and say where you think they were taken.

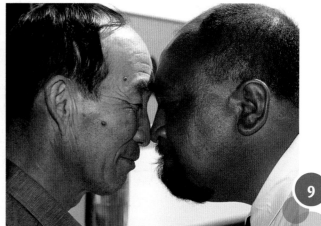

What should you say? What should you do?

● Are you good in social situations? Can you always think of the right thing to say?

Reading

1 Answer the questions in the quiz. Then compare your answers with a partner.

Are you a good guest?

You're visiting a friend's family in another country.
What would you say in each situation?

1 You want to know whether
to take your shoes off before
you go into the house.
a) Should I take my shoes
off?
b) I don't need to take my
shoes off, do I?
c) Do you want me to take my shoes off?

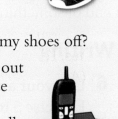

2 Your mobile phone has run out
of credit and you want to use
the landline.
a) I need to make a phone call.
Where's the phone?
b) Could I use the phone, please?
c) Can I use the phone?

3 You are about to have
dinner, but you're not
sure where to sit.
a) Where would you
like me to sit?
b) Where should I sit?
c) I'll sit here, shall I?

4 Your friend's parents are
in the kitchen preparing
a meal.
a) I'm really hungry!
b) Need any help?
c) Can I help you?

5 You're having dinner and you
want the salt, but you can't
reach it.
a) Pass the salt.
b) May I have the salt, please?
c) Can you pass the salt?

6 Your friend's coughing and
can't stop.
a) Would you like
a glass of water?
b) You should drink
some water.
c) Be quiet!

Scoring

Work out your score.

1	a 3	b 1	c 2
2	a 1	b 3	c 2
3	a 3	b 2	c 1
4	a 1	b 2	c 3
5	a 1	b 3	c 2
6	a 3	b 2	c 1

Analysis

6–9   Perhaps you should have stayed at home.

10–13   You're fine.

14–18   Well done! You'll definitely get another invitation!

Use of English: Modals

Modal verbs are 'auxiliary' verbs like *shall, should, can, could, will, would, may, might*. We use them before main verbs, for example, when asking for advice or permission.

Asking for and giving advice
Should I take off my shoes?
You should drink some water.

Permission
Can I use the phone?
Could I use the phone, please?

Note: *could* and *may* are more formal than *can*.

Offering to do something
Can I help you?

Requests
Can you pass the salt?
May I have the salt, please?

2 Complete the conversations using modal verbs. There may be more than one possibility.

A Have you got everything you need?
B I'm sorry, but I've forgotten my towel.
   (*Ask to borrow one.*)
   May / Could / Can I borrow one?

A Did you have anything to eat on the journey?
B Well, not much.
A (*Offer to make a sandwich.*)

A Do you want to let your parents know you've arrived safely?
B Yes, please. (*Ask to use the computer to send an email.*)

B I feel quite tired after the journey. I can't keep my eyes open!
A (*Give advice.*)

A Do you want to get anything to take home?
B Yes, I'd like to buy a present for my parents.
   (*Ask for advice.*)

Listening 3

3 Read these expressions. What are they in your language?

Congratulations!	Goodnight, sleep well.	Well done!
Happy New Year!	Have a good holiday.	Have a good weekend.
Nice to meet you.	See you later.	Welcome to _____

4 Listen to the scenarios and respond with an appropriate expression from Exercise 3.

Speaking

5 Work in pairs. Make up and roleplay five short dialogues, like the ones you've just heard. In each dialogue, include one of the expressions from the box in Exercise 3.

It's better to give than to receive

- Look at the pictures. What can you say about each one?

Reading

a

b

c

Famous gifts in history

1 The Greeks and the Trojans had been at war for ten years. To bring the war to an end, the Greeks had a brilliant idea. They built a wooden horse and left it at the gates of Troy as a gift for the Trojans. The Greeks sailed away. The Trojans pulled the horse into their city as a victory trophy, but they didn't know that there were Greek soldiers hiding inside the horse. During the night, the soldiers got out of the horse and opened the city gates for the rest of the Greek army, which had sailed back to Troy during the night. …

2 The Statue of Liberty was a gift to the United States of America from the people of France in 1886. It was given to celebrate the centenary of the American Declaration of Independence (4th July 1776). The statue, designed by Frédéric Bartholdi, is of a woman holding a torch. The statue itself is over 46 metres tall. …

3 The Rothschild Fabergé Egg was a gift from Beatrice Ephrussi to Germaine Halphen, when she became engaged to Beatrice's younger brother, Baron Edouard de Rothschild, in Paris in 1902. The egg is made of pink enamel and gold; on the front is a clock. Every hour, a cockerel set with diamonds pops up from inside the egg, flaps his wings four times and then nods his head three times. It remained in the Rothschild collection for over a hundred years. …

4 China's use of giant pandas as diplomatic gifts has a long history, dating from the seventh-century Tang Dynasty, when Empress Wu Zetian sent a pair of pandas to the Japanese emperor. From 1958 to 1982, China gave 23 pandas to nine different countries. …

d

1 **Answer the questions.**

1 Which picture goes with each piece of text?
2 What do the gifts in pictures b and d have in common?
3 What do the gifts in pictures a, b and c have in common?
4 Which gift was not really a gift?

12

2 Choose the correct sentence to complete each paragraph on page 12.

a There is a broken chain at her feet.

b In 2007, the family sold it for 18.5 million US dollars.

c They were hugely popular and were an enormous diplomatic success.

d They entered the city and destroyed it, bringing the war to an end.

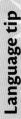

Language tip

When you read, you can get a general idea of what a text is about, but you might not understand every word. Try to work out the meaning of unfamiliar words from their context; for example, 'gift'. The article is called 'Famous gifts in history' and it's about things that people have given to each other on special occasions. So a gift is something that you give on a special occasion. If you can't work out the meaning, use a dictionary.

Listening 4

3 Listen to two people talking on a radio programme. What are they talking about? Which country do they mention?

4 Listen again and answer the questions.

1 What should you take when you visit friends and family?

2 Should you be careful when giving flowers? Why?

3 How should you wrap your gifts?

4 When is money a suitable present?

5 Is there anything you should remember when giving money?

6 What do you give to close friends and family?

7 When do you open your gifts?

8 When do you exchange gifts?

Speaking

5 Work with a partner. Ask and answer the questions in Exercise 4 with reference to gift-giving in your country.

Project: A guide to social customs

6 Design and write a guide to social customs for an exchange student visiting your school.

• Work in groups. First discuss the following questions and write down all your ideas.

1 What do you do when you meet someone for the first time? Are there different customs for greeting people of different ages?

When you greet an older person, for example a grandparent, you _____

When you meet an adult, you smile and shake hands. You shouldn't _____

2 How should children address their teachers? *They should call them* _____

3 What do visitors need to know about gifts? *When you visit someone, you can take* _____

• Now plan your guide. Decide which ideas you're going to use.

• Decide who is going to write each section.

• Design and write your guide.

- **Topics** Life at school; describing someone in your family; family history
- **Use of English** The present perfect for situations continuing up to now; apostrophes *'s* and *s'*

So far, so good

- What are the main differences between your secondary school and your primary school? Think about the subjects you do, the school day, the size of the school, the classrooms and activities outside lessons.

Reading

1 A teacher has asked new students to describe their first few weeks at secondary school. Read what two of them said. Are they mostly positive or negative about their new school?

2 Answer the questions.
1 How long have Shamira and Sunil been at their new school?
2 What problems have they had?
3 What do they say about friends?
4 What does Shamira think may happen after half-term?
5 What do you think Shamira means by 'so far, so good'?
6 Which activity does Sunil do outside lessons?

First impressions

Blog spot

▶ Posted by: <u>Shamira</u>, Year 7

My first few weeks at secondary school have been really fun! I've made loads of new friends and I've also met up with some old friends that I haven't seen for a while, so that's been good. At first, it was hard to find all my classes – I kept getting lost and one teacher told me off because I was ten minutes late for her lesson. Now I know my way around. The teachers have been really kind and the lessons aren't too difficult. We haven't had much homework yet, but I'm sure we'll get more after half-term. Anyway, so far, so good!

▶ Posted by: <u>Sunil</u>, Year 7

On my first day here I was a bit nervous, but after a few hours I was fine. The first few weeks have been really good. I've enjoyed learning new subjects and making new friends. My favourite subject is Science. It's fun learning in a lab! I've joined the school orchestra. I play the drums. It's great. We're doing a concert at the end of term.

Listening (5)

3 Before you listen, read the questions in the survey. Who do you think wrote the survey? Who is going to answer it?

4 Listen to Shamira and Sunil doing the survey. Have they done well at school this term?

5 How did Shamira and Sunil answer each question? Listen again.

Class survey

This term ...

1 Which subjects have you enjoyed most?

2 Which subjects have you enjoyed least?

3 What have you done in Science?

4 What have you done in History?

5 Have you had good marks in all subjects?

6 Have you done any after-school activities?

7 Which sports have you played?

8 Have you been in trouble? And what for?

9 Has the headteacher spoken to you?

10 Have you enjoyed this term so far?

Use of English: Present perfect simple

Present perfect simple	Remember
We use the present perfect to talk about situations continuing up to the present.	We use the past simple to talk about situations which have ended.
Which subjects have you enjoyed this term?	Which subjects did you enjoy last term?
I've enjoyed Science.	I enjoyed Maths.
Has the headteacher spoken to you?	

Language tip

We also use the present perfect when we don't specify a past time.

What have you done in Science?

We've done the human body.

6 Complete the sentences using the present perfect of the verb in brackets.

1 I*'ve made* a lot of new friends this term. *(make)*

2 I think we _____ _____ too much science homework this term. *(have)*

3 I _____ _____ new subjects like Technology and Design. *(enjoy)*

4 I'm in the football team, but we _____ _____ any matches yet. *(not play)*

5 My friend _____ _____ in trouble with the headteacher. *(be)*

6 _____ you _____ the science labs? They're great! *(see)*

Speaking

7 With a partner, ask and answer the questions in the class survey.

You and your family

- What do you know about your grandparents' early lives? Do you know anything about your great-grandparents?

Great-grandparents?

How many cousins have I got?

How much do *you* know about *your* family?

1 What are your grandparents' first names?

2 Where were your parents born?

3 How many brothers and sisters did your grandparents have?

4 Where were your great-grandparents born?

5 What is your father's date of birth?

6 How many aunts and uncles have you got? What are their full names?

7 How many cousins have you got? Can you name them all?

8 Have you got any relatives you've never met?

9 Have any members of your family emigrated to other countries? Who, and where?

10 Are there twins in your family? If so, are they identical?

JULIA

ROBERTO

SARA

JORGE

OK, I'll pretend to be you and you can pretend to be me.

Vocabulary

1 Look at the questions in the quiz on page 16. Find the words for:

1 mother and father *parents*
2 your parents' parents
3 your uncle's wife

4 your aunt and uncle's children
5 people from the same family
6 brothers and sisters of exactly the same age

Speaking

2 With a partner, ask and answer the questions in the quiz. Which ones are hard to answer? Is there any way you can find out the missing information?

Use of English: Apostrophes 's and s'

Notice the difference between apostrophe s ('s) and s apostrophe (s'):

- apostrophe s ('s) shows that something belongs to one person or one thing

- s apostrophe (s') shows that something belongs to more than one person or thing.

What is your father's date of birth? = What is the date of birth of your father?
What are your grandparents' first names? = What are the first names of your grandparents?

Why is the apostrophe before the s in the first sentence and after the s in the second sentence?

---

3 Put the apostrophes in the right position in these sentences.

1 My cousins name is Su-Wei. *cousin's*
2 My grandmothers name is Aisha.
3 When I was young I lived very near my grandparents house.

4 The twins hair is not the same colour as their fathers hair.
5 My fathers brothers live in Jakarta.
6 I enjoy finding out about other peoples family histories.

Writing

4 Read this description of a family. Then answer the questions.

1 What's the name of the person who wrote it?
2 How many aunts and uncles has she got?
3 Who are Rosa and Natalia?

5 Use the description in Exercise 4 to write a similar description of your own family.

> My grandmother's name was Alicia and I'm named after her. She was my father's mother. My father has got two brothers and two sisters and my mother has got three brothers and a sister. I've got more than twenty cousins. I've met most of them, but not all of them. Two of my cousins are about the same age as me. Their names are Rosa and Natalia. I get on very well with them. We have a lot of fun when we get together at their house.

Family history

- How do people find out about their family history?

Reading and speaking

1 Look at the map and read the article to find out about a scientific approach to family history. What does the map show?

A **remarkable** journey

"I'm from Poland and my parents, grandparents and great-grandparents are Polish too. It was really interesting to find out that my family history starts in Africa. The DNA test showed that, over time, my ancestors travelled from Africa to north-eastern Europe. They were part of a group which also travelled as far east as India and Pakistan. I had no idea! This has helped me understand one simple thing: we are all one big family!" *Luiza*

"I was amazed to find out that my ancestors travelled through eastern Europe on their way to India, where I was born. Suddenly I felt connected with countries like Hungary, Romania and the Czech Republic. Before this, they were only names on a map to me." *Raju*

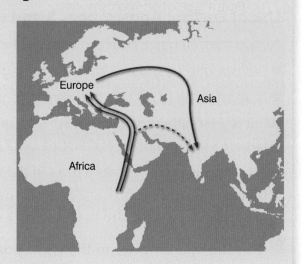

2 Find these words in the text. Choose the correct meaning.

1 **remarkable**   **a** long and difficult   **b** very unusual in a way that you admire
2 **ancestors**   **a** important people in history   **b** people in your family a long time ago
3 **amazed**   **a** confused   **b** very surprised
4 **connected with**   **a** distant from   **b** joined to

3 Answer the questions.

1 On the map, which is Luiza's ancestors' route? Which is Raju's?
2 Have Luiza's family lived in Poland for a long time? How do you know?
3 What nationality is Raju?
4 What surprised Luiza and Raju about their ancestors?
5 What can your DNA tell you about your family?

4 Work in pairs. Ask and answer these questions.

1 What do you know about your family history?
2 Has your family always lived in the same area?
3 Are you named after anyone in your family?
4 Who is the oldest person in your family? Tell me about him / her.

5 Read Cecilia's profile of her great-grandmother. Look at the second sentence: *She's my father's grandmother.* What does the first apostrophe show? What does the second apostrophe show?

Writing

6 Write a profile of the oldest person in your family. Use Cecilia's profile to help you. Check what you've written. Make sure you have used the apostrophes correctly.

Project: A report for your school magazine or website

7 Write a report for your school magazine or website about your impressions of school so far this term. Use the plan below to help you. Illustrate your report with photos and drawings

The oldest person in my family is my great-grandmother. She's my father's grandmother. Her name is Giulia. She's 96 and she was born in Naples, in Italy. She had seven brothers and sisters.

When she was 18, she emigrated to Argentina with two of her brothers. She's lived here for 78 years and she's never been back to Italy, but she still speaks Spanish with an Italian accent!

I've got some cousins and other relatives who live in Italy. I haven't met them, but I'd love to meet them one day.

Cecilia, Buenos Aires, Argentina

> **Language tip**
>
> When you're writing about people, you can join sentences together by using *who*:
>
> *I've got some cousins and other relatives. They live in Italy.*
>
> *I've got some cousins and other relatives <u>who</u> live in Italy.*

Paragraph 1		**Paragraph 3**	
General impresssion	So far this term has been …	*After-school activities*	I've joined … /
The first few days	On my first day, …		I've played …
	At first, …	**Paragraph 4**	
Paragraph 2		*Conclusion*	I've enjoyed science lessons
School subjects	My favourite subject is …		and I've enjoyed doing
and homework	It's fun (learning / doing) …		Drama.
	In Science / History, we've …		I've made some new friends
	We've had quite a lot of		here.
	homework in … , but not		So far, so good!
	much in …		

Stage 1	Write your report.	**Stage 3**	Check your spelling and punctuation.
Stage 2	Read your report and check your grammar. Have you used the present perfect correctly?	**Stage 4**	Write a final version of your report.

Fiction

1 Do you like humorous books or do you prefer serious ones? Give some examples of books you've enjoyed.

2 Read the introduction and the extract. Do you think *Hullabaloo in the Guava Orchard* by Kiran Desai is a humorous book or a serious book?

> The story is set in Shahkot, a small town in India. It's about a boy called Sampath. His father, Mr Chawla, has ambitions for him and wants him to do well in life. But Sampath is not interested in having a job and getting married. He's a dreamer.
>
> The following scene takes place in the morning. Sampath has taken a long time over his breakfast; he has been watching a fly on some fruit. Sampath's grandmother, Ammaji, is busy preparing lunch boxes for Sampath and his father to take to work.

Hullabaloo in the Guava Orchard

"Phoo!" Mr Chawla snorted. "Progress! Ever since he was born, this boy has been progressing steadily in the wrong direction. Instead of trying to work his way upwards, he started on a downward climb and now he is almost as close to the bottom as he could ever be."

"But the world is round," said Ammaji, pleased by her own cleverness. "Wait and see! Even if it appears he is going down hill, he will come up out on the other side. Yes, on top of the world. He is just taking the longer route."

"He is not taking any route, I tell you. He has missed the route altogether. He is just sitting by the side playing with flies." Mr Chawla turned back to Sampath, who had closed his eyes, imagining a long and peaceful sleep in a cool dark place. "Come on," his father urged him. "Get ready for work. It's nine o'clock. Why are you still sitting here like a potato?" He twitched with impatience. "What is the matter with this family? I am the only one with any sense of responsibility, any idea of the way things work in this world. If it wasn't for me, Sampath would be sitting in a special museum for people who are a cross between potatoes and human beings." In the tone of a tour guide, he intoned: "Watch how this peculiar vegetable spends its day." And, to show just what he thought of the way this peculiar vegetable spent its day, he picked up his lunch box and marched, each footstep firm and loud, down the stairs on his way to work.

From *Hullabaloo in the Guava Orchard*
by Kiran Desai, Faber & Faber, 1998

3 Match the words and phrases to their definitions.

1	snorted	a	containing the qualities of two different things
2	steadily	b	a person who shows tourists interesting places and things
3	urged	c	made a loud noise by forcing air out through the nose, like a horse
4	twitched	d	made a sudden short nervous movement
5	a cross between	e	said slowly and clearly without changing his tone of voice
6	tone	f	slowly and gradually
7	tour guide	g	strange, unusual, often in a bad way
8	intoned	h	walked like a soldier
9	peculiar	i	the quality of a sound, especially someone's voice
10	marched	j	strongly advised

4 Answer the questions.

1 Why is Mr Chawla impatient with Sampath this morning?
2 Where is Mr Chawla going?
3 Why does Sampath close his eyes?
4 How would you describe Mr Chawla's attitude to Sampath?
5 How would you describe Ammaji's attitude to Sampath?
6 What impression do we get of Sampath?
7 Give two examples of how the writer uses humour in this extract.

Discussion

5 Work in groups. Discuss these questions.
Do you know anyone like
Mr Chawla, Sampath or Ammaji?
How are they similar? How are
they different?

Review of Units 1–2
Vocabulary
Meeting and greeting

1 Make six phrases for meeting and greeting using the words in the circle.

1 How's it going?

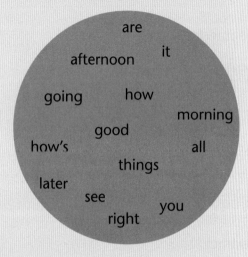

are
afternoon
it
going
how
morning
good
how's
all
things
later
see
you
right

2 Complete the phrases with the correct verb.

1 n_____ your head
2 b_____ your head
3 sh_____ hands
4 p_____ your hands together
5 g_____ someone a kiss on the cheek

3 Match the words from the two columns to make phrases.

1 Sleep well

1 Sleep   a done
2 Well   b later
3 Happy   c meet you
4 Have   d New Year
5 Nice to   e well
6 See you   f a good holiday

4 Use five of the phrases from Exercise 3 to respond to what these people say.

1 - I wish I was coming with you!
  - *Have a good holiday.*
2 - I'm going to school now. Bye.
  - _____ .
3 - I've passed my Grade 5 exam.
  - _____ .
4 - Hello, I'm Saleh.
  - _____ .
5 - Goodnight.
  - _____ .

School

5 Fill in the missing words.

1 I play in the volleyball team and the football team, I'm in the chess club and I play in the school orchestra. I do a lot of *after-school* activities!
2 Maths and Science are my favourite school _____ .
3 The school day starts at 8.30. We have five _____ and each one lasts 50 minutes.
4 I don't mind working in the evening, but I think we have too much _____ .
5 I like History a lot, but I get my best _____ in English.

6 Adapt each sentence in Exercise 5 so that it is true for you.

Family

7 Identify the family members.

1 Your uncle's wife   *aunt*
2 Your mother's brother
3 Your mother and father
4 Your parents' parents
5 Your uncle and aunt's son or daughter
6 People in your family a long time ago
7 Your parents' parents' parents

Use of English

8 Complete the sentences with *should / shouldn't, can / can't, could* or *may*.

1 *Ask for advice*
(we / write) in our books or in our notebooks?

Should we write in our books or in our notebooks?

2 *Give advice*
(you / not work) too late the night before an exam.

3 *Ask for permission*
(I / leave) early today, please?

4 *Offer to do something*
(I / help) you carry those books?

5 *Make a request*
(you / close) the door, please?

9 Rewrite these sentences putting the apostrophe in the correct place.

1 My friends brother is a footballer.

My friend's brother is a footballer.

2 Our headteachers name is Mrs Smith.

3 Our science teachers names are Mr Hassan and Mrs Vidal.

4 My parents apartment is above their shop.

5 Australias flag is red, white and blue.

10 Write six sentences saying what you've done or haven't done so far this week.

Here are some ideas:

I've seen my cousins. / I haven't seen my cousins.

- see my cousins
- visit my grandparents
- watch a football match on TV
- do all my homework
- play the piano / guitar / drums …
- tidy my room
- go swimming
- read a book
- have a pizza

General knowledge quiz

11 Work with a partner. Ask and answer the questions.

1 What did the Greeks leave as a gift for the Trojans at the gates of their city, Troy?

2 What was inside the Greeks' gift to the Trojans? What happened?

3 Look at the photo. What is it?

4 The Statue of Liberty was a gift from one country to another. Which were the countries?

5 What kind of animal did China give to several countries between 1958 and 1982?

6 In India, what colour flowers should you <u>not</u> give as a gift?

7 In India, when do people give money as a present?

8 Put the letters in the correct order to make the names of two continents:
F A R I C A   U P E O R E

9 It's in the nucleus of cells and it contains genetic information. What is it?

10 Name two countries in eastern Europe.

3 Clothing and accessories

- **Topics** clothes and fashion; the clothes and accessories of the ancient Egyptians; an advert for an accessory
- **Use of English** phrasal verbs; present passive, including modals with passives (*it can be worn*)

How important are clothes to you?

- What's your favourite item of clothing? Why?

Vocabulary

1 Read the descriptions of six items of clothing. Do you know what each one is? Find the names for them in the circles on the right.

B E R R M O
M R O R A O K I
O S I S O N

A S R T A N
A M J I T H D N A
Y P S H B A

1 Men, women and children wear this traditional item of clothing. Its name means 'thing to wear' in Japanese. It has long, wide sleeves. It doesn't have buttons or a zip. You wrap it around your body, always with the left side over the right, and tie it at the back with a sash. Today, it's worn mainly on special occasions.

2 The word comes from Persian and means 'leg garment'. Originally they were loose trousers, tied at the waist, and they were worn by men and women in south and west Asia. Today, they are worn all over the world, usually to sleep in.

3 Its name comes from its shape. It's usually made of cotton and has short sleeves. It was originally worn under a shirt, for warmth. It doesn't have a collar. Now it's worn all over the world, either with a shirt or without a shirt, and often with jeans.

4 It's a hat which comes from Mexico. You wear it to protect you from the sun. The word comes from the Spanish for 'shade' or 'shadow'.

5 This word comes from the Sanskrit word meaning 'to tie'. It's a large colourful handkerchief which is worn on the head or around the neck. Today, it's sometimes worn by tennis players.

6 This word also comes from Sanskrit and it means 'strip of cloth'. It's a long piece of material which is wrapped around the waist and then goes over the shoulder. It's popular in many Asian countries, such as India, Pakistan, Nepal, Malaysia and Singapore. It's worn by women and girls.

Did you know? Sanskrit is an old language of India. It's used in literature and some religious writings. Words in English which have come from Sanskrit include *rice, sugar, orange, yoga, vivid*. Can you think of any words in English which have come from your language?

2 Find the words for the items in the picture. They are all in the text in Exercise 1.

 a
 b
 c
 d
 e

Reading

3 Read what Amani and Will say about clothes and fashion.

> I love fashion and I love shopping for clothes. I go window-shopping with my friends and sometimes we go into the shops just to try things on. For real shopping I go with my mum. When I get something new I put it on as soon as I get home and I put on a bracelet or a necklace to see what looks good with it. I always fold my clothes and put them away carefully or I hang them up in my wardrobe. I love dressing up for special occasions.
>
> *Amani*

> I don't follow fashion and I'm not interested in designer clothes or what celebrities wear. At home at the weekend, I wear an old pair of tracksuit bottoms, but I don't go out in them! My favourite item of clothing at the moment is my black T-shirt. When I go out, I wear it with jeans and a pair of bright yellow trainers. I'm not very good at looking after my clothes. When I go to bed, I just take them off and throw them on the floor.
>
> *Will*

4 Answer the questions about the text. Who …

1 enjoys shopping and trying on clothes?
2 isn't interested in fashion?
3 likes jewellery and accessories?
4 has a tidy bedroom?
5 doesn't put things away?
6 likes to wear comfortable clothes at home?

5 Use the words in the box to complete the phrasal verbs in the following questions.

on (x 2)	off	for	up (x2)	away

1 Do you enjoy shopping _____ clothes?
2 Do you always try clothes _____ before you buy them?
3 Do you like dressing _____ for special occasions?
4 In the morning, when you get dressed, do you always put your clothes _____ in the same order?
5 When you take your clothes _____ at the end of the day, do you put them _____ carefully and hang them _____ in a wardrobe?

Use of English: Phrasal verbs

Phrasal verbs are verbs made up of two or more words; for example, *get up, look at, sit down.*

Find some examples of phrasal verbs in the texts in Exercise 3.
to shop for clothes

When the object of a phrasal verb is a noun, you can put the two words of the verb together or you can separate them.
I put on a bracelet.

OR
I put a bracelet on.
But if the object is a pronoun, you must separate the two words.
I put it on.

NOT
I put on it.

Speaking and writing

6 Ask and answer the questions in Exercise 5 with a partner.
Then write a paragraph giving your views on clothes and fashion.

What's it made of?

- What colours do you like wearing? What's your favourite item of clothing made of? Do you ever wear jewellery?

Reading

1 What do you know about the ancient Egyptians? What clothes did they wear? What kind of accessories did they have? Read the text and find out.

2 Find the following in the text.

- one type of footwear   *sandals*
- two items of clothing
- four items of jewellery
- two other accessories

3 Are these sentences true or false?

1 Ancient Egyptians wore a lot of linen.
2 Only women wore skirts.
3 Men wore make-up.
4 Everyone wore sandals.
5 Yellow and green were important colours for the ancient Egyptians.
6 The Egyptians liked wearing black clothes.
7 Accessories were important to the ancient Egyptians.
8 Their accessories were practical rather than decorative.

CLOTHING AND FOOTWEAR

The most popular material for clothes was linen. The men wore skirts with a belt. The women wore long, straight dresses. Both men and women wore make-up and jewellery. Only the Pharaoh and people of high status had footwear. They wore sandals with leather straps.

Colours were symbolic for the Egyptians. Yellow symbolised gold, green was the symbol of youth and life, black was only for wigs and white was the symbol of happiness.

JEWELLERY

People have always worn jewellery to show off their status, for decoration, for practical purposes, or just for fun. In the land of the Pharaohs, accessories were a status symbol. The ancient Egyptians are well known for being the first to make jewellery on a large scale. They liked to use gold for their bracelets, rings, earrings, decorated buttons and necklaces.

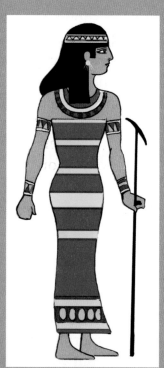

Speaking

4 Work in pairs. Ask and answer the questions.

1 What accessories do you have with you every day?
2 Are there any accessories you wear or have with you on special occasions?
3 Have you got any jewellery? When do you wear it and why?
4 Is jewellery more important for girls than for boys? Give a reason for your answer. Was it different in the past?

Vocabulary

5 **Where do these materials come from? Complete the sentences.**

- cotton
- wool
- silk
- leather
- gold and silver
- plastic

1 *Silk* is made from fibres produced by *silk* worms.
2 _____ is a cloth that is made from the _____ plant
3 _____ comes from sheep and other animals such as alpacas and vicunas.
4 _____ is made from an animal's skin.
5 _____ is made from oil.
6 _____ are found in rocks in the ground.

6 **Complete these sentences using the present passive.**

1 Wigs _____ of horsehair, hair or synthetic fibre. (*make*)
2 A violin bow_____ of wood and horsehair. (*make*)
3 Diamonds _____ at high temperature deep underground. (*form*)
4 Belts _____ of leather, plastic or cotton. (*can / make*)
5 Baseball caps and sunglasses _____ in the classroom. (*should / not / wear*)

Speaking and listening (6)

7 **With a partner, try this quiz. Ask all three questions about each item of clothing. Then listen and check.**

A *I'll ask the questions about kimonos and saris and you ask the questions about lederhosen and kilts.*
B *OK. You start.*
A *Where are kimonos worn?*

QUICK QUIZ: **CLOTHES** FROM **AROUND THE WORLD**

kimonos   saris   lederhosen   kilts

1 Where are they worn?
2 What are they made of?
3 Who are they worn by? (women? men? children?)

> **Language tip**
>
> Note the difference between *made of* and *made from*:
> This jacket *is made of* linen.
> Linen *is made from* flax. Flax is a plant which grows in the Nile area.

> **Use of English: Present passive**
>
> We use the present passive when we want to talk about an action, but we don't know who does it, or it's not important to say who does it.
> *Plastic is made from oil.*
>
> verb *be*   past participle
>
> *Silver and gold are found in rocks in the ground.*
>
> How do you make the present passive?
>
> You can also use words like *can*, *should* and *must* with the present passive:
> *Sunglasses should be worn in strong sunlight.*
> *A mobile phone can be used as a torch.*

Writing

8 **Choose two of the items of clothing in Exercise 7 and write a paragraph about them. Listen again if necessary.**

The most useful accessory you'll ever buy!

● Describe an advert you've seen. Why do you think you remember it?

a    b    c

d    e    f

Reading

1 These adverts describe three of the items above. Which are the items?

1 **You'll never** get lost when you're wearing these stylish trainers because there's a GPS tracker in the right shoe which is powered by a battery in the left shoe. Attractive, practical footwear with the latest technology – what more could you want?

2 **This is** a state-of-the-art helmet for skiers and snowboarders who want to listen to their favourite music as they zoom down the slopes. It can also be worn for other outdoor sports where protection for the head is needed.

3 **You're going** on a trip. You need your phone, your camera, your laptop … but how are you going to charge the batteries? Easy. Just take this neat backpack with a built-in solar-powered charger.

Listening ⑦

2 Listen to the adverts and match the descriptions to the pictures.

Speaking

3 What can you remember about the solar-powered baseball cap, the jacket and the trainers? Listen again. With a partner, ask and answer about each item.

1 What's special about it/them?
2 When and where would you use it/them?

Project: Give a presentation of a product

4 Work in small groups. Look at the picture. Why do you think this is the most useful accessory you'll ever buy? Read and find out.

Product information

The most useful accessory you'll ever buy!

It can be used as a neckerchief, headband, mask, hair tie, bandana, hairband, balaclava, scarf, wristband, cap, pirate-style cap, …

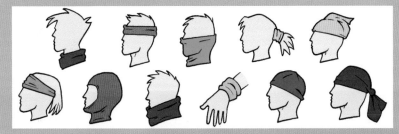

Features of this product:

It is available in a variety of designs and colours.

It is simple and versatile.

It can be worn in at least ten different ways.

It is comfortable to wear.

It can be machine washed.

It can be customised with your own design.

Millions are sold every year.

It weighs less than 60 grams.

The product is made of polyester microfibre.

It measures 50cm by 23cm when it is laid out flat.

One size fits most adults, junior size is available.

Helps to protect against the cold, sun, wind and dust.

When it is folded, it will easily fit into your pocket.

When it is washed, it dries in minutes and keeps its shape.

6 You're going to present this product to your teacher.

Use the product information to make notes for your presentation under the following headings:

What is it?

It's an accessory which can be used …

- **Size and technical specifications**
- **Style**
- **Practical points**
- **Sales**
- **End with a simple message**

7 Decide who is going to present each aspect of the product. Use a computer program, such as PowerPoint, to help you present the product.

We're going to talk to you today about a fantastic new product. What is it? Over to you (Jasmine).

Well, it can be used as a _____

5 In your opinion, what are the best things about this product? How would you use it?

Outdoor pursuits

- **Topics** Outdoor sports and activities in New Zealand; activity holidays; school trips
- **Use of English** The present perfect with *ever*; expressing the future; *-ing* forms as subjects, objects and after a preposition

The land of adventure

- Where is New Zealand? What do you know about it?

Reading

1 Read the information about outdoor activities in New Zealand. Is the information mainly about the North Island or the South Island? How are the two islands different?

Did you know? The Maoris were living in New Zealand before the Europeans arrived in the seventeenth century. The Maori name for their country was 'Aotearoa', meaning 'land of the long white cloud', but the Europeans called it New Zealand. Has your country always had the same name?

From trekking to sky diving – NEW ZEALAND HAS IT ALL

Seventy per cent of New Zealanders live on the North Island, but the South Island is full of places to explore.

Start in Queenstown, known as the 'Adventure Capital of the World' because it offers every outdoor pursuit you can think of: snowboarding, bungee jumping, paragliding, zorbing and more. North-east of the city is Lake Wanaka, where all sorts of activities are on offer: walking, trekking, mountain biking, fishing, sailing, kayaking, water skiing, white-water rafting, sky diving, canyoning …

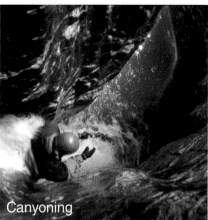
Canyoning

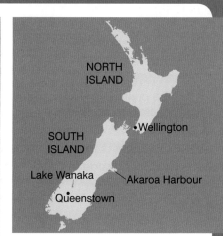

NORTH ISLAND

•Wellington

SOUTH ISLAND

Lake Wanaka

Akaroa Harbour

Queenstown

Zorbing

Have you ever swum with dolphins? No? Well, make your way to Akaroa Harbour, where you can swim with the world's smallest dolphins. At the end of the day, explore the Te Anau Glowworm Caves, where you will see underground waterfalls and more. Then, in a small boat, you will visit a dark area of the caves, where thousands of glowworms live and light up the space.

SAFETY FIRST

- Your safety is our business.
- All activities are organised by qualified instructors.
- For some activities, children must be accompanied by an adult.

Listening 🔵8

2 Listen to Alana telling her mum about New Zealand. What is Alana's attitude to outdoor pursuits and what does her mum think about them?

3 Listen again. What are these outdoor pursuits?
1 bungee jumping   3 zorbing   5 sky diving
2 paragliding   4 white-water rafting   6 canyoning

Vocabulary

4 Find all the outdoor pursuits in the text in Exercise 1. List them under three headings: Land, Air and Water. (Some can go under more than one heading.)

Speaking

5 Test your partner. Take it in turns to choose an activity from the lists in Exercise 4. Describe the activity without naming it. Your partner has to say what it is. You can use dictionaries or other resources to help you.

A *It's a winter sport and you do it on snow. It's a bit like skiing.*
B *Is it snowboarding?*
A *Yes, it is. OK, your turn.*

6 Use the prompts to ask and answer about the sports and activities.

- try   snowboarding / paragliding / sky diving / zorbing
- do   a bungee jump / a parachute jump
- swim   with dolphins
- see   an underground waterfall / glowworms

A Have you ever tried snowboarding?

B Yes, I have.   B No, I haven't.

A Tell me about it.   A Would you like to?

B The last time I went, …   B Yes, I would. / No, I wouldn't.
  What about you?
  Have you ever … ?   A Why? / Why not?

          B Because … . What about you? Have you ever … ?

> **Use of English: Present perfect with *ever***
>
> To ask about experiences (things you have done), use the present perfect with *ever*.
>
> *Have you ever swum with dolphins?*
> *Yes, I have. / No, I haven't.*
>
> *Has Alana ever been to New Zealand?*
> *Yes, she has. / No, she hasn't.*

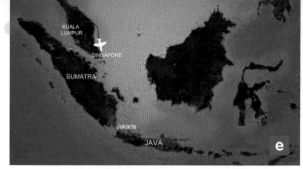

Alana goes to New Zealand

- How would you travel to New Zealand from your country? How long would it take?

Reading

1 Look at the following messages and pictures (a–j). Answer the questions.

1 How many emails are there? How many text messages? What else is there?

2 Who is going on a journey? Who is she going to visit?

2 Put the items a–j in Exercise 1 in the correct chronological order.

1 i

Listening 🔟 9

3 Listen and check.

4 Answer these questions.

1 When is Alana going to New Zealand?

2 Which outdoor pursuits does she want to try?

3 What will she need when she goes surfing?

4 What's the weather going to be like?

5 Where is the plane when the pilot speaks to the passengers?

6 Where will Paula be waiting for Alana?

a ☒

Hi Alana

You won't need any special equipment. It's all provided. And you won't need waterproof stuff – we've got lots here and in any case it'll be summer. But bring a wetsuit if you've got one because we'll be surfing at Whale Bay!

Paula

b ☒

Hi Alana

I'm really pleased that you're coming. We'll have a great time!

Love Paula

c I've just checked on the Internet and your plane's on time. I'm leaving for the airport now and I'll be waiting for you in the coffee bar near where you come through from the baggage reclaim. See you soon. Paula

d ☒

Hi Auntie Paula

What shall I bring with me? What's the weather going to be like? Am I going to need wet-weather gear? I want to go kayaking and white-water rafting. Do I need to bring a helmet and a life jacket?

Love Alana

f

Skate & Surf Shop

BB Plaza, Kuala Lumpur

1 wetsuit

Price: MYR 400.00

Total to pay: MYR 400.00

g I'm just waiting for my bag to come through. See you in a minute. Alana

h ☒

I've got a wetsuit, I've packed my bag, I've checked in online and I've got my boarding pass, so I'm all set.

Alana

i ☒

Hi Auntie Paula

I'm coming to see you in December. Mum's just booked the ticket. I leave on 21st and I arrive on 22nd. I can't wait!

Love Alana

j ☒

Thanks, Auntie Paula. I haven't got a wetsuit, but we're going to get one tomorrow.

Alana

Use of English: Expressing the future

There are several ways of talking about the future in English. Rather than trying to learn the rules, just memorise some key examples, like the ones below.

Present continuous

• for fixed arrangements
  I'm coming to see you in December.

going to

• for plans and intentions
  We're going to get one tomorrow.

• for predictions based on what you know or what you can see
  What's the weather going to be like?
  (Look at those clouds. It's going to rain.)

will / shall

• for giving information about the future
  It'll be summer.

• for predicting what we think or guess will happen
  We'll have a great time!

• for asking or suggesting what to do (use *shall*)
  What shall I bring with me?

Present simple

• for timetables and schedules
  I leave on 21st.

Future continuous

• saying that something will be in progress at a time in the future
  We'll be surfing at Whale Bay.

5 Find more examples of the future in the messages in Exercise 1. Where do they go in the *Use of English* box above?

6 Choose the best option.

1 A: What are you doing next Saturday?
  B: I (*go* / *'m going*) mountain biking.
  I'm going mountain biking.
2 I've just seen the weather forecast. It (*isn't going to* / *doesn't*) rain tomorrow.
3 What do you want to do next weekend?
  (*Shall* / *Will*) we go fishing?
4 I've looked at the timetable. The train (*leaves* / *is going to leave*) at 9.30.
5 Just think – this time next week we'll (*surf* / *be surfing*) at Whale Bay!
6 The beaches are fantastic there. You (*will* / *shall*) have a great time.

Speaking

7 With a partner, discuss your plans for the next few days.

A *What will you be doing at this time tomorrow / at 2 o'clock on Saturday afternoon / on Saturday evening / at 9 o'clock on Sunday morning?*

B *I'll be playing tennis. What about you? What will you be doing?*

Planning a school trip

- Have you ever been on a school trip? Where was it? What was it like? Where would you like to go on your next school trip?

Vocabulary

1 Complete the list using the words in the box.

> making   cooking   following
> identifying   putting up

Outdoor survival skills

1 _____ a tent
2 _____ a campfire
3 _____ over a campfire
4 _____ a path or a trail
5 _____ trees, plants and wildlife

2 Match the words in the two columns.

1b a pair of trainers

You will need to bring:

1	a pair of	a	costume
2	a sleeping	b	trainers
3	a waterproof	c	clothes
4	a change of	d	bag
5	a swimming	e	trunks
	or	f	jacket
6	swimming		

Listening 10

3 Imagine that you are going to an activity centre with your class tomorrow. What information does your teacher need to give you?

4 Listen and answer the questions.

1 Who are the people in this conversation?
2 What is the conversation about?

Lakeside Activity Centre

Learn to survive in the great outdoors, enjoy some **exciting** watersports and take a trip through the treetops!

zip lining

windsurfing

follow a nature trail

5 Listen again and complete the notes about the school trip.

School trip to Lakeside Activity Centre

Day 1

Meet at school at: _____ am

Coach departs at: _____ am

Morning activities: _____

Lunch: sandwiches and a drink

Afternoon activities:

(1) _____

(2) forest trail activities – following a trail and identifying trees and plants and wildlife

OR _____

Supper: 6.00 pm _____

Evening activities: story telling and singing round the campfire

Lights out: 9.30 pm

Day 2

Breakfast: _____ am

Morning activities: _____

Lunch: 12.30 pm

Afternoon activity: _____

Coach leaves at: _____ pm

Use of English: -ing forms

We use -ing forms (verb + -ing) in English where some other languages use infinitives. Look at the examples. How would you say these sentences in your language?

-ing forms as subjects
Putting up a tent is easy.

-ing forms as objects
I don't like falling into the water.

-ing forms after a preposition
I'm no good at putting up tents.

Writing

6 Use words ending in -ing to complete these sentences, so that they are true for you.

1 … is easy / difficult.   *Riding a bike is easy.*
2 … is fun.
3 I don't like …
4 I enjoy …
5 I'm good at …
6 I'm no good at …

Project: Planning a school trip

7 Work in groups. Plan a two-day school trip.

- Decide where to go. Think of the activities you can do.
- Use the schedule in Exercise 5 to help you write a plan of your trip.
- Prepare a talk about your trip. If possible, find some pictures to illustrate your talk.
- Divide the talk into sections. Each person in the group takes a section to talk about.

A *We're going on a trip to … .*
B *You'll need to be at school at … because we'll be leaving at … from … .*
C *When we get there, the first thing we'll do is … .*

8 Give your talk to the class. Members of the class can interrupt with questions:

What's the weather going to be like?
What will I need to bring?
What will we be doing in the evenings?

Poetry and song

1 Read this postcard poem. What kind of trip is Ben on? Is it a day trip or is he staying longer? How do you know?

Postcard from School Camp

Dear Mum and Dad,

                   Weather's poor, food's bad, teachers are grumpy, instructors are mad. Cramped in tent, cold at night, no dry clothes, boots too tight. Didn't like canoeing, the hiking was tough, all in all I've had enough.

        Bye for now, MAY see you soon

         If I survive this afternoon

            Your loving son,

              Ben xx

P.S. Can I come again next year?

P.S. = *post scriptum* (Latin meaning 'after having written') – a note at the end of a letter adding something you've forgotten to say.

'Postcard from School Camp' by Richard Caley, from *The Works*, Macmillan Children's Books, 2010

2 Choose the correct meaning of these words.

1	grumpy	**a** in a good mood	**b** in a bad mood
2	cramped	**a** not much space	**b** comfortable
3	tight	**a** too big	**b** too small
4	hiking	**a** walking long distances	**b** climbing mountains
5	tough	**a** easy	**b** difficult
6	survive	**a** stay alive	**b** enjoy

3 Answer the questions.

1 What do you learn about Ben's trip from his postcard?
2 Why do you think the information in the postcard is written in note form rather than in complete sentences?
3 Why has the poet chosen to write a poem that looks like a postcard message?
4 Where do the rhyming words usually appear in a poem? Where do they appear here?
5 Why is the P.S. a surprise?

4 Work with a partner. Find the words that rhyme in the postcard poem and practise saying them.

5 Practise and perform the poem in pairs like this:

A *Postcard from School Camp*
B *Dear Mum and Dad,*
A *Weather's poor, food's bad,*
B *teachers are grumpy, instructors are mad.*
A *Cramped in tent, cold at night,*
B *no dry clothes, boots too tight.*
A *Didn't like canoeing, the hiking was tough,*
B *all in all I've had enough.*
A *Bye for now, MAY see you soon*
B *If I survive this afternoon*
A *Your loving son,*
B *Ben xx*
A *P.S. Can I come again next year?*

6 When students go on a school trip, they often sing songs. Read the words of this song. Is it a serious song or a comic song?

> **Forty Years on an Iceberg**
>
> Forty years on an iceberg
> Out on the ocean wide
> Nothing to wear but pyjamas,
> Nothing to do but slide
> The wind was cold and icy,
> The frost began to bite
> I had to hug a polar bear
> To keep me warm at night!
> La la la la …

7 Find the words in the song for the following:

1 a large piece of ice that floats in the sea
2 measuring a distance from one side to the other
3 move smoothly over a surface
4 white icy powder that you see on trees and plants in very cold weather
5 a type of animal that lives in the Arctic

8 On a school trip, when and why do you think you would sing this song?

9 Practise and perform the song. Use these actions to illustrate the meaning.

Line 1: Make 10 four times with your fingers.
Line 2: Make a wave movement with your hand.
Line 3: Pretend to button your pyjamas.
Line 4: Make a sliding movement with your feet.
Line 5: Shiver with your arms around you.
Line 6: Bite your teeth together.
Line 7: Pretend to hug a polar bear.
Line 8: Smile to show that you're now warm.

Review of Units 3–4
Vocabulary
Clothing and accessories

- backpack
- belt
- bracelet
- buttons
- earrings
- necklace
- collar
- ring
- sleeve
- wig
- zip

1 Read the definitions. Find a word in the box for each one.

1 You wear them on your ears. *earrings*
2 This is useful for carrying things.
3 You wear it around your waist.
4 It's a kind of jewellery which you wear on your wrist.
5 It's a kind of jewellery which you wear around your neck.
6 You wear this on your finger.
7 This is made of hair.
8 They're usually round and they keep parts of a shirt together.
9 It's part of a shirt or a jacket which covers the whole or part of your arm.
10 This keeps two parts of an item of clothing together.
11 It's the part of a shirt or a jacket which goes around your neck.

Materials

2 What materials can the following be made of? Give examples.

1 a warm coat *wool*
2 jeans
3 a scarf
4 a belt
5 a ring or earrings

Outdoor pursuits

3 Write the words under the correct heading.

kayaking	mountain biking	trekking
snowboarding	windsurfing	sailing
skiing	fishing	waterskiing
surfing	swimming	

water	snow	land
kayaking		

4 Which sport is it? Choose from the list above.

1 You do this in the sea, but without a boat or a sail. If it's cold, you wear a wetsuit. *surfing*
2 You do it on snow, but you don't use skis.
3 You do this on water. You have a boat, but it hasn't got a sail.
4 You travel through the water by moving your arms and legs.
5 You need a boat to pull you through the water and you should wear a life jacket.
6 You walk long distances.

Use of English

5 Write the correct preposition in each sentence.

1 When you get dressed, do you always put your clothes *on* in the same order?
2 Do you enjoy shopping _____ clothes and accessories?
3 Do you always try clothes _____ before you buy them?
4 Do you like dressing _____ for special occasions?
5 When you take your clothes _____ at the end of the day, do you put them _____ carefully?

6 **Rewrite the following sentences using the passive.**

1 We invite you to a welcome party on the first evening of your stay.

   You are invited to a welcome party on the first evening of your stay.

2 We serve breakfast from 7.30 to 9.30.

3 We ask guests to leave their keys at reception.

4 We sell items, such as soap, shampoo and toothpaste, at reception.

5 You can order a packed lunch.

6 You must not wear walking boots in the hostel.

7 **Choose the correct option.**

1 The film (*starts* / *will start*) at 7 o'clock. Don't be late.   starts

2 I (*'ll see* / *see*) you tomorrow outside the cinema at 6.45 pm.

3 The weather forecast is really good. It (*isn't going to* / *doesn't*) rain tomorrow.

4 This time next week, we'll (*be enjoying* / *enjoy*) a meal at my uncle's restaurant.

5 I didn't do well in my last spelling text, so I'm (*doing* / *going to do*) really well in the next one.

8 **Correct these sentences.**

1 I'm interested in learn survival skills.

   I'm interested in learning survival skills.

2 We're thinking of go on a camping holiday next year.

3 I like be outdoors.

4 I'm no good at put up a tent.

5 Sing around a campfire will be fun.

6 I think I'll enjoy cook over a campfire.

7 I'm not afraid of sleep in a tent.

8 I like read in bed, so I'll have to take a torch.

9 Are you good at follow a path or a trail?

10 Ride a mountain bike along the forest trails will be great.

General knowledge quiz

9 **Work with a partner. Answer the questions.**

1 It comes from sheep and other animals. You can use it to make warm clothes. What is it?

2 Its name means 'thing to wear' in Japanese. What is it?

3 Which old language of India do the words 'rice', 'sugar' and 'yoga' come from?

4 Who wore sandals in ancient Egypt?

5 Look at the picture of the ancient Egyptians. What can you say about the colours they are wearing?

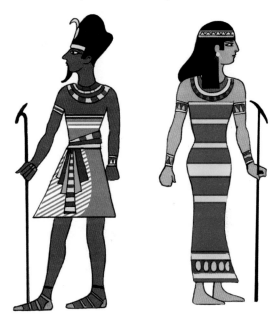

6 Which material comes from flax, a plant which grows in the Nile area?

7 Where do men and boys wear kilts and what are kilts?

8 Its Maori name means 'land of the long white cloud'. Which country is it?

9 Who are the Maoris?

10 This sport involves travelling down a fast-flowing river in an inflatable boat. What is it?

- **Topics** Transport systems around the world; the history of transport; road signs and road safety
- **Use of English** Past simple passive; *wish (that)* + past simple

Getting from A to B

- What's your favourite way of travelling?

Vocabulary

1 Play this game with a partner.

- Describe one of the following types of transport without using the word.
- Your partner has to guess what it is.

What is it?

BUS TRAIN SPEEDBOAT
VAN TAXI
BIKE SHIP
TRACTOR CANOE
RAFT
FERRY CAR
SCOOTER TRAM PLANE
LORRY
MOTORBIKE
TUK TUK HELICOPTER
SNOWMOBILE

A *It's got wheels and it takes people from one place to another.*
B *Is it a car?*
A *No, it isn't. It's got three wheels and the passengers sit behind the driver.*
B *Is it a tuk tuk?*
A *Yes, it is!*

2 What do these photos show?

Reading

3 Match each paragraph to a photo.

Transport systems around the world

1 The buses in Curitiba, a city in southern Brazil, carry two million passengers a day – that's 85% of the city's population. You buy your ticket before you get on the bus: the fare is the same wherever you're going. No one in the city lives more than 400 metres from a bus stop. Buses are very frequent and the tube-shaped bus shelters are raised to make it easy to get on and off the bus. People don't need to use their cars in the city, so there's less pollution and less congestion.

2 The first metro stations in Moscow were built in the 1930s and 1940s as 'palaces for the people'. The architecture was grand and the decoration was elaborate. Komsomolskaya station, for example, had marble colums, mosaics and chandeliers, which you can still see today. The metro carries 7 million passengers a day on weekdays and is known for being frequent and reliable.

3 Japanese bullet trains travel at up to 320 kilometres an hour. The 520-kilometre journey between Tokyo and Osaka, the world's busiest high-speed line, takes just three and a half hours; by car, it would take seven. Bullet trains are used by commuters because they're fast, reliable and punctual. They're popular with foreign tourists, too, because, as a tourist, you can buy a rail pass which gives you unlimited travel during your trip to Japan.

4 Copenhagen was recently voted 'the world's best cycle city'. A third of the people who live there commute to work by bike. In fact, you see more bikes than cars in the city centre. There are 350 kilometres of cycle paths; some of them are raised above the level of the road. You don't even need to have your own bike; you can use a city bike, which is free.

5 A good way to travel in Singapore is by river taxi. It's not expensive and you get a great view of the city from the river. Water taxis are popular with commuters, tourists and anyone who wants to get from A to B. Each taxi can carry up to 60 passengers.

Vocabulary

4 Find words for the following in the text.

1 Someone who travels, but is not the driver of the vehicle.   *passenger*
2 The price you pay to travel.
3 A place where you wait for a bus.
4 The place where a metro train stops.
5 Someone who regularly travels between home and work.
6 Someone who travels for pleasure.
7 A ticket which you can use for several journeys.
8 Part of the road set aside for bikes.

5 Answer the questions.

1 Why is the bus fare system in Curitiba easy to understand?
2 Why is the Curitiba bus system good for the environment?
3 What was special about the first metro stations in Moscow?
4 Where would you normally expect to find:
   a marble columns?
   b mosaics?
   c chandeliers?
5 Why might a foreign tourist pay less than a commuter to travel on a Japanese bullet train?
6 Is the Copenhagen bike scheme popular? How do you know?
7 What are the advantages of travelling by river taxi in Singapore?

Speaking

6 With a partner talk about the advantages of …

1 the buses in Curitiba
2 the Moscow metro
3 the bullet train in Japan
4 bikes in Copenhagen
5 the river taxi in Singapore

Boats, buses and balloons!

- In your country, how did people travel 200 years ago?

Vocabulary

1 Match the captions to the pictures.

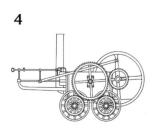

a the first car
b a canal with a lock
c a boat with a sail
d a steam railway locomotive
e an omnibus with an open upper deck
f a raft made of bamboo

Reading

2 Read the article and write a heading for each paragraph.

A brief history of PUBLIC TRANSPORT

The earliest form of public transport was water transport. Boats and rafts made of reeds, wood and animal skins were used as ferries in places as far apart as Egypt and South America. In about 4000 BCE, boats with sails were used in Mesopotamia (now Iraq) and by 2000 BCE, the Egyptians had boats with a single square sail that travelled along the River Nile.

Early Chinese engineers built canals for carrying boats. The Grand Canal was begun in 485 BCE and was completed in 1283. It was 1780 kilometres long. Canal locks were first used from about 500 BCE, also in China. The first important canal in Europe was the Canal du Midi in France, completed in 1681.

The railway age began in Britain with Richard Trevithick's steam railway locomotive in 1814. The first passenger railway was opened in 1825 in the north of England. At first, people were worried that they wouldn't be able to breathe while travelling so fast – the first trains reached speeds of 25 kilometres per hour! The coming of the railways revolutionised travel. Long-distance railways opened up the USA and Canada; remote farming areas in India and South America were linked with major ports.

The first buses were introduced in France in 1827 by Stanilas Baudry. They were pulled by horses and they were called *voitures omnibus*. Omnibuses in London in 1850 could carry up to about 20 passengers. Within a few years, an open upper deck was added to carry more passengers. Travelling on the upper deck was charged at half fare. Road travel changed forever when the first motor car was built by Karl Benz in 1885. Horse-drawn buses disappeared; they were replaced by buses with petrol engines. And, of course, cars began to take over the roads.

3 Make a timeline showing a brief history of public transport, using the information in the text above.

4000 BCE	2000 BCE	1885
boats with sails, Mesopotamia	...	...

Use of English: Past simple passive

We use the past passive when we want to talk about an action, but we don't know who did it, or it's not important to say who did it.

| was / were | past participle |

The Grand Canal was begun in 485 BCE.

If we want to say who did the action, we use the passive with *by*:

The first buses were introduced in France in 1827 by Stanilas Baudry.

In this sentence the action (the introduction of buses) has more importance than the person (Stanislas Baudry), so it comes first.

4 Make these sentences passive. You don't need to say who did the action.

1 They completed the Canal du Midi in 1681.
The Canal du Midi was completed in 1681.
2 They opened the first railway in 1825.
3 They linked remote farming areas with major ports.
4 People called the first buses *voitures omnibus*.
5 They added an upper deck to carry more passengers.

5 Make these sentences passive. Use *by* to say who or what did the action.

1 Horses pulled the buses. *The buses were pulled by horses.*
2 Stanilas Baudry introduced the first buses in France in 1827.
3 Karl Benz built the first car in 1885.
4 Buses with petrol engines replaced horse-drawn buses.

Listening 11

6 Work in groups of three. Listen to an account of the first hot-air balloon flights. Student A, make notes in answer to these questions:

1 Where was the first hot-air balloon made?
2 What was the balloon made of?
3 How was it held together?
4 What was the box below the balloon made of?
5 When was the first balloon flight?
6 How long did the flight last?
7 How far did the balloon travel?

Student B, make notes in answer to these questions:

1 What colour was the second Montgolfier balloon?
2 What was in the basket attached to this second balloon?
3 Where was the demonstration performed?
4 Who was the demonstration watched by?
5 How long did this second balloon flight last?
6 How far did this second balloon travel?

Student C, make notes in answer to these questions:

1 When were the first people sent up in a balloon?
2 How long did this third flight last?
3 Which city did it fly over?
4 How far did this third flight travel?
5 What two things were designed to look like balloons?

7 Now ask each other the questions. Use your notes to answer.

Writing

8 In the same groups of three, use your answers to the questions in Exercise 6 to write an account of the first hot-air balloon flights.

How streetwise are you?

● Think of the road signs near your school. Do they give you information or do they warn you of danger?

Reading

1 What do you think these signs mean?

2 Read the definitions. Then complete the collocations using the words in the box.

> parking path limit bumps
> one-way pedestrian lights
> entry

1 You must stop when the light is red: traffic *lights*
2 Drive slowly over these: speed _____
3 You can't go down this street in a car: no _____
4 Only bikes, not cars, are allowed here: cycle _____
5 You can cross the road on foot here: _____ crossing
6 You can only drive in one direction in this street: _____ street
7 You can't leave your car here: no _____
8 You mustn't go faster than this: speed _____

3 Work in pairs. Draw signs for five of the warnings in Exercise 2. Show your signs to another pair of students and ask them to guess what they are.

4 Design your own road sign and ask other students to guess what it means.

5 Write the missing labels on the plan. Look at Exercise 2 to help you.

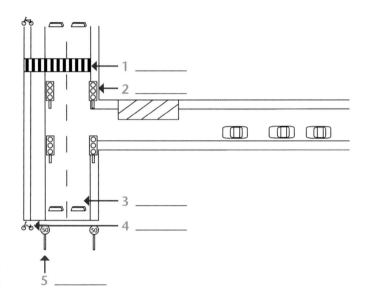

Listening 12

6 Think of the roads near your school. What are the problems for pedestrians, cyclists and drivers?

7 Listen to the headteacher and students on the school council having a discussion. What are they talking about?

8 Listen again and answer these questions.
1 How many problems does the headteacher identify?
2 Why is there congestion near the school?
3 Where are the traffic jams?
4 Why is cycling on Garden Road dangerous?
5 Where is the nearest bus stop?

9 Before the meeting with the school council, the headteacher asked all students to make a 'wish list'. Here are some of the things they wrote.

> I wish we had a cycle shelter for our bikes.

> I wish I could cycle to school. I wish there were proper cycle paths.

> I wish I didn't have to walk to school.

> I hate waiting for the bus in the rain. I wish there was a bus shelter.

> I wish I could come to school by helicopter.

10 Find the past tense verbs in the sentences in Exercise 9.

I wish we <u>had</u> …
I wish I <u>could</u> …

> **Use of English: *wish (that)* + past tense**
>
> After *wish (that)*, the past tense is used.
>
> *I wish we had a cycle shelter for our bikes.*

Writing

11 Write a 'wish list' for your school. Remember to use the past tense after *I wish (that)*.

somewhere to play football

a swimming pool

seats or benches in the playground

a games room with a table tennis table

Project: Getting to and from school

12 What would make your journey to and from school easier? Work in groups.

1 Student A: Draw a plan of the area around your school, like the one in Exercise 4.
2 Student B: Label the plan.
3 All: Discuss your ideas for improving travel to and from your school.
4 Student B: Add the ideas to the plan.
5 Student C: Present the ideas to the rest of the class using the plan to illustrate them.

Decide who is going to do each task, like this:

> Who's going to draw the plan? You're good at drawing …

> Shall I do the labelling?

> I could do a PowerPoint presentation, if you like.

6 Using maps

- **Topics** Street maps and transport maps; map reading; mountain rescue
- **Use of English** Prepositions to do with travel; comparative adjectives using *much … than, (not) as … as*; past continuous

Finding your way

- What are the points of the compass? Have you got a good sense of direction?

Vocabulary

1 How many words can you think of for places or buildings in a town or city?

hotel, bank, …

2 Look at the maps on these two pages.

- Which cities are shown?
- Who would find these maps useful?

Listening 13

3 Look at the maps and then listen to the conversation. In which city is Mark lost?

4 Listen again. Find the places on the map and answer the questions.

1 Where is Mark?
2 What can he see on the left?
3 What can he see straight ahead?
4 Where is Anya?
5 Which building is she near?
6 What are Anya and Mark going to do?

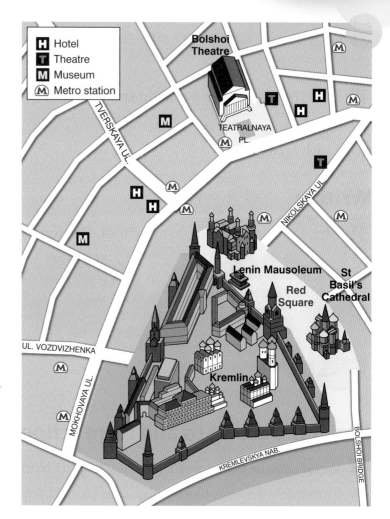

5 Complete the summary using the prepositions in the box.

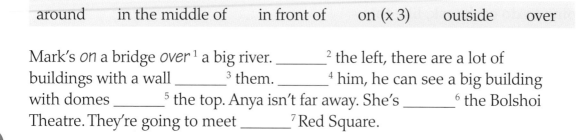

| around | in the middle of | in front of | on (x 3) | outside | over |

Mark's *on* a bridge *over*¹ a big river. _____² the left, there are a lot of buildings with a wall _____³ them. _____⁴ him, he can see a big building with domes _____⁵ the top. Anya isn't far away. She's _____⁶ the Bolshoi Theatre. They're going to meet _____⁷ Red Square.

6 **14** Listen and trace Linda's route on the subway map.

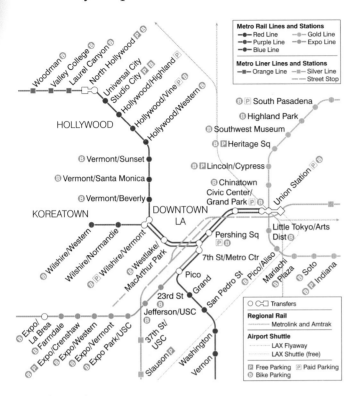

7 Which of these expressions did you hear in the phone conversation? What do the expressions mean?

Sorry, you're breaking up.
Sorry, what did you say?
I didn't quite catch that.
Thanks for calling.
Speak to you later.

Writing

8 Write down the details of the conversation.

Means of transport: _____
Which lines? _____
Change at: _____
Destination: _____
Reason for journey: _____

Use of English: Prepositions to do with travel

I'm **on** the subway.

I'm coming **into** Chinatown.

Where do I change **to/for** the Red Line?

You just change **at** Union Station.

It's the stop **after** Chinatown.

Where do I get **on/off** ?

9 Complete the conversation with the correct prepositions.

A Hi, I'm _____¹ the Blue Line train. How do I get to Highland Park?

B Where are you now?

A The train's just coming _____² Vernon.

B OK. You need to get _____³ the subway, so change at 7ᵗʰ Street / Metro Center to the Red Line.

A Great, that's easy.

B But then you have to change again _____⁴ Union Station to the Gold Line.

A OK. And where do I get _____⁵?

B At Highland Park. It's the stop _____⁶ Southwest Museum.

Speaking

10 Work in pairs. Select one of the maps and choose two places or stations on the map. Have a phone conversation about how to get from one place to another. Include some of the phrases from Exercise 7.

A *Hi, where are you?*
B *I'm at . . . . Where are you?*
A *I'm outside / in the middle of / on / at . . . .*
B *How do I get to . . . ?*
A *Sorry, I didn't quite catch that.*

How to read a map

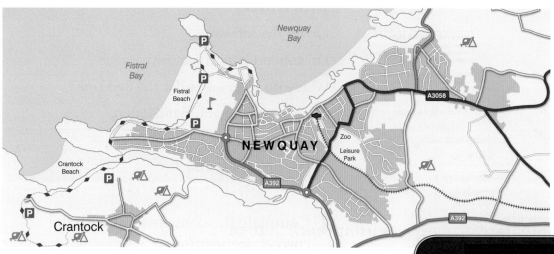

Conventional map

Satellite map

- What can a map tell you?

Vocabulary

1 Use the map of Newquay to match the symbols to their meaning.

Tourist information

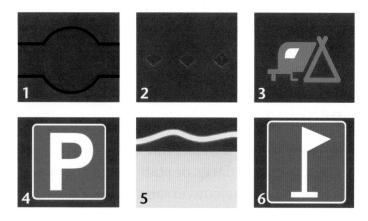

a car park
b long-distance path
c golf course
d beach
e railway station
f caravan site

2 Look at the maps and answer these questions.

1 Is there a town or a city? What is it called?
2 Is the area inland or on the coast? How do you know?
3 What can you say about the coast?
4 Is the railway station far from the beach?
5 What are the dark green areas on the satellite map?
6 Do you think this is a holiday area or an industrial area? Give reasons for your answer.

Reading

3 Read the opinions about using maps. Which do you agree with?

> A satellite map isn't as clear as a conventional map. But it gives you a better idea of what things look like.

> It's much easier to understand a map when you know what all the symbols mean.

> I think a conventional map is much better and much more useful than a satellite map when you're trying to find your way around because the detail is much clearer.

> I just can't read a map. You can show me where I am on a map, but I can't work out from the map how to get to another place. I think it's much better to ask people for directions.

Use of English: Comparative adjectives using *much ... than* and *(not) as ... as*

Use comparative adjectives to make comparisons: *smaller than, bigger than*

- Most one-syllable adjectives make their comparative by adding *-er*: *clear – clearer*
  Sometimes you have to make spelling changes: *easy – easier*

- For longer adjectives, including some two-syllable adjectives, use *more* + adjective:
  useful – more useful   important – more important

- To make a comparison stronger, use *much*:
  It's much easier to understand a map when you know what all the symbols mean.
  A conventional map is much better and much more useful than a satellite map.

- To make a comparison between things that are or aren't equal, use *(not) as ... as*:
  A satellite map isn't as clear as a conventional map.

4 With a partner, look at the map again and complete these questions using comparative adjectives. Then answer them, using *much* where possible.

1 Which beach is *closer* to the railway station, Fistral Beach or the beach at Newquay Bay? (*close*)
   The beach at Newquay Bay is much closer than Fistral Beach.
2 Is Fistral Beach _____ than the beach at Newquay Bay? (*long*)
3 Is Crantock _____ as Newquay? (*big*)
4 Is the golf course much _____ than Fistral Beach? (*big*)
5 You're going from the campsite at Crantock to Fistral Beach. Is it _____ to go by car than it is to go on foot? (*convenient*)

Speaking

5 Work with a partner. Use the prompts to give your opinions using *much ... than*, and *(not) as ... as*. Then exchange opinions with other pairs.

1 Having a holiday at the beach / exciting / visiting a big city.
   Having a holiday at the beach is much more exciting than visiting a big city.
2 Camping / enjoyable / staying in a hotel.
3 Finding your way with a map / reliable / asking people for directions.
4 A compass / useful / a mobile phone when you're walking in the mountains.
5 Visiting a big modern city / interesting / visiting a small old town.
6 Travelling by train / quick / travelling by bus.

A lucky escape

- What should you do to be safe when you're skiing, snowboarding or walking in the mountains?

Saved by the light of a
mobile phone

A snowboarder was feeling lucky to be alive yesterday after a dramatic helicopter rescue.

Ben Akintola, 30, was snowboarding in the French Alps under a clear blue sky when an avalanche started. He didn't have time to escape and it hit him with full force and knocked him unconscious.

He woke in the middle of the night in pitch darkness. He was lying on a narrow, icy ledge. Amazingly, he still had a mobile phone signal, so he called a friend a thousand kilometres away in Britain. His friend called the French rescue services.

"I was waiting for what seemed like hours on that narrow ledge. I was beginning to give up hope when I heard the sound of a helicopter. It was circling around in the darkness, looking for me. I was waving my mobile around desperately. Fortunately the helicopter pilot saw the light."

"I was overjoyed when the helicopter headed my way. It hovered above me and began lowering a rope."

Ben was in hospital last night but he was not being treated for any serious injuries. He's looking forward to going home today.

The French rescue services said: "We were very pleased that we were able to rescue Ben. The risk of avalanches off-piste is much higher at this time of year. All snowboarders and skiers should stay on the ski runs and not go off-piste. Ben had a lucky escape."

Reading

1 Read the newspaper article. Which of the following are implied in the text?

1 Ben was unconscious for several hours. *This is implied because we know that the avalanche happened during the day, when the sky was blue. But Ben woke in the middle of the night.*

2 It's not always easy to get a mobile signal in the mountains.

3 Ben used the torch on his mobile phone to attract the pilot's attention.

4 Ben wasn't seriously hurt.

5 Ben was snowboarding off-piste.

6 Ben was snowboarding with friends when the accident happened.

7 Ben won't try off-piste snowboarding again.

Language tip

A writer doesn't always state things directly. Sometimes meaning is 'implied': the writer suggests something is true or that something happened, without actually saying it.

Use of English: Past continuous

- We use the past continuous when we want to say that something was happening around a particular time in the past.

  past tense of *be*   verb + *-ing*

  He woke in the middle of the night in pitch darkness. He was lying on a narrow, icy ledge.

- We often use the past continuous in narrative descriptions:
  A snowboarder was feeling lucky to be alive yesterday after a dramatic helicopter rescue.

- We can also use the past continuous and the past simple together to show that one action interrupted another:
  He was snowboarding in the French Alps under a clear blue sky when an avalanche started.

How many more examples of the past continuous can you find in the newspaper story?

- Note that there is a passive form of the past continuous:
  Ben was in hospital last night, but he was not being treated for any serious injuries.

Listening 15

2 Listen to the radio report of Ben's rescue and compare it with the newspaper report. There are six pieces of information that are different. What are they?

newspaper report

1 There was a clear blue sky.
2 Ben was snowboarding.
3 He was lying on a narrow icy ledge.
4 The helicopter pilot saw the light from Ben's mobile phone.
5 Ben wasn't being treated for any serious injuries.
6 He was in hospital for one night.

radio report

It was snowing heavily.

Project: Write a newspaper article

3 Write an article similar to the one in Exercise 1 about the following rescue.

SAVED BY A MAP AND A MOBILE

Eighteen-year-old Lara Moore had a lucky escape yesterday.

Fiction

1 Read this introduction. Why do some stories remain popular for a long time?

> *One Thousand and One Nights* is a collection of stories from three cultures – Indian, Persian and Arab. The first stories came from a book of Persian fairy tales which were translated into Arabic in about 850 CE. Stories such as *Aladdin* and *Sinbad the Sailor* are now known all over the world.
>
> The person who tells the stories is a young woman called Shahrazad. She has to tell the king a story every night in order to escape death.

2 Now read *The Dream*. Does it have a happy ending?

3 Match the words and phrases to their definitions.

1	merchant	a	a place where criminals are kept
2	careless	b	a very hard stone used for statues and for buildings
3	fortune	c	an open space surrounded by walls or buildings
4	to afford	d	something good in the future or a very large sum of money
5	courtyard	e	not careful
6	to break into	f	a person who buys and sells things
7	prison	g	someone you don't know
8	stranger	h	to be able to pay for
9	to burst out	i	to be put under the ground
10	marble	j	to go into a building to steal something
11	to be buried	k	to make a hole in the ground
12	to dig	l	to suddenly start

4 Answer the questions.

1 Why did the merchant leave Baghdad?
2 Where did he go?
3 Why did he sleep in the courtyard of a mosque?
4 What happened while he was sleeping?
5 Why did the police put him in prison?
6 Why did the Chief of Police laugh at the merchant?
7 How did the Chief of Police help him?
8 What did the merchant find when he got home?

5 Work in groups. Retell the story without looking at the text.

6 Work in groups. Answer these questions.

1 Why are stories about dreams popular with writers and readers?
2 In the story, did the Chief of Police really have a dream about the merchant's house in Baghdad? What do you think?
3 Does *The Dream* have a 'moral' (a message) or is it just a story?

The Dream

There was once a merchant who lived in Baghdad. He had a lot of money, but he was careless with it and over time he lost it. He became very poor.

One night, as he lay in bed with a heavy heart, a man came to him in a dream and said: 'Your fortune is in Cairo. Go and find it there.'

The next morning, when he woke up, he remembered his dream. What should he do? He decided to set out on his long journey. After many weeks on the road, he came at last to Cairo. It was night-time. He could not afford a place to sleep, so he lay down in the courtyard of a mosque and soon fell asleep.

As he was sleeping, some robbers broke into a house next to the mosque. The people in the house cried for help, but by the time the police arrived, the robbers had gone. The police found the merchant from Baghdad in the courtyard of the mosque and put him in prison. Three days later, the Chief of Police told his men to bring the stranger to him.

'Where do you come from?' asked the Chief.

'From Baghdad.'

'And why have you come to Cairo?'

'A man appeared to me in a dream, saying: "Your fortune is in Cairo. Go and find it there." But when I came here to Cairo, my fortune was to be put in prison.'

When he heard this, the Chief of Police burst out laughing. 'I must tell you that I too have heard a voice in my sleep, not just once, but three times. It said:

"Go to Baghdad and in a street with palm trees on both sides you will find a certain house, with a courtyard of grey marble; at the end of the garden there is a fountain of white marble. Under the fountain, a great sum of money is buried. Go there and dig it up." Did I go? Of course not! But you, you fool, have come all the way to Cairo just because you had a silly dream!'

Then the Chief of Police gave the merchant some money. 'Here,' he said, 'take this. It will help you get back to your own country.' The merchant realised at once that the house and the garden that the Chief of Police had described were his own. He took the money and set off quickly on his journey home.

As soon as he reached his house, he went into the garden. He dug under the fountain and found the treasure described by the Chief of Police. He was rich once again.

From *One Thousand and One Nights*

Review of Units 5–6

Vocabulary

Transport

1 How many types of transport can you think of that:

a go on water?   *ship*
b go on rails? _____
c have four or more wheels? _____
d have two wheels? _____

2 Match the words in the two columns to make compound nouns (nouns of two or more words).

bus fare, bus shelter, …

1	bus	a	bumps
2	railway	b	fare
3	cycle	c	lights
4	one-way	d	limit
5	traffic	e	park
6	speed	f	path
7	car	g	shelter
		h	station
		i	stop
		j	street

3 Find compound nouns from Exercise 2 to match these sentences.

1 Don't go at more than 50 kilometres per hour.   *speed limit*
2 Catch your train here.
3 Leave your car here.
4 Stop when you see red.
5 Wait for your bus here or here.
6 It's safer to use this when you go by bike.
7 Go slowly over these.
8 You can only go in one direction here.

4 Write a definition of each person.

1 commuter   4 passenger
2 tourist   5 pedestrian
3 cyclist   6 pilot

A commuter is a person who travels some distance to and from work every day.

Use of English

5 Complete the text by changing the verbs in brackets into the past simple passive.

THE EARLY HISTORY OF THE BICYCLE

The bicycle (*invent*) **was invented**[1] by the German Karl von Drais in 1817. It had two wheels, but no pedals. You pushed it along with your feet. It (*know*) _____[2] as the 'draisine' after its inventor and it (*make*) _____[3] of wood. The word 'bicycle' appeared in the 1860s when it (*use*) _____[4] to replace the French name *vélocipède à pédales*.

Pedals (*add*) _____[5] to the front wheel of the bicycle in 1864. The first inflatable rubber tyres for a bicycle (*invent*) _____[6] by a Scottish man called John Dunlop in 1888.

6 Write each sentence as a thought beginning *I wish* …

1 The bus is always late.
2 There's so much traffic.
3 I can't cycle to school.
4 There isn't a cycle path between my house and the school.
5 I have a double Science lesson today.

> I wish the bus wasn't always late.

7 Complete the dialogue with the correct prepositions.

on	after	into	off	at	for

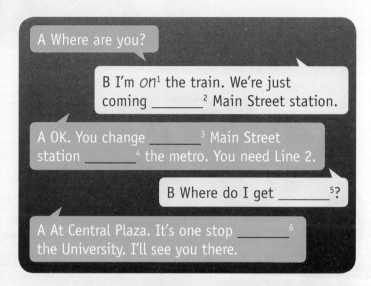

A Where are you?

B I'm *on*[1] the train. We're just coming _____ [2] Main Street station.

A OK. You change _____ [3] Main Street station _____ [4] the metro. You need Line 2.

B Where do I get _____ [5]?

A At Central Plaza. It's one stop _____ [6] the University. I'll see you there.

8 Past simple or past continuous? Match the questions and the answers.

1 What did you do after school yesterday?
2 Why didn't you answer your phone?
3 Where did you go last weekend?
4 Where were you when I texted you?
5 Did your cousins do anything special last weekend?
6 Why didn't your cousins come on the camping weekend?
7 Why did you all go to bed so late?
8 What did you all do after dinner?
9 How did you find your way here?
10 Why did you fall over?

a I was looking at the map.
b I looked at a map.
c We were singing songs round the campfire.
d We sang songs round the campfire.
e They had a family party.
f They were having a family party.
g I watched TV.
h I was watching TV.
i I was going to the beach.
j I went to the beach.

9 Make comparisons with *much … than* and (*not*) *as … as* using the information given.

1 Use *much*.

Cars	
Fiat 500	BMW 7
3545.84mm	5024mm

The BMW 7 is much longer than the Fiat 500.

or

The Fiat 500 is much shorter than the BMW 7.

2 Use *much*.

Bikes	
Road racing bike	Mountain bike
6.3 kilos	14.06 kilos

3 Use *much*.

Ships	
Carnival Dream	Oasis of the Seas
3646 passengers	5400 passengers

4 Use *almost as …* .

Trains	
AVE (Spain)	Frecciarossa (Italy)
356km per hour	340km per hour

5 Use *not as …* .

Motorbikes	
Harley-Davidson	Suzuki
$14,000	$15,000

7 Health, food and exercise

- **Topics** A balanced diet; getting enough exercise and sleep; the diet and training of Kenyan long-distance runners
- **Use of English** Quantifiers with countable and uncountable nouns (*a few, a little* …); adjectives and adverbs; comparatives of adverbs; position of adverbs of frequency

A balanced diet

- What's your favourite dish, and what are the ingredients? Are there any foods that you don't like?

Reading

1 Read the information. Why is the title 'Food for life'?

2 Look at the picture. How many food groups can you see? Which foods contain the following?

| protein | carbohydrates | fat | sugar |

Which food group in the picture do we need to eat most of? Why?

FOOD for life

Protein is used to build our bodies and to make them strong. It can be found in meat, fish, eggs, nuts and pulses.

Carbohydrates give us energy and can be found in bread, pasta and rice, for example.

We need **fat** to keep us warm and to protect us.

Sugar gives us quick energy, but we should try to eat it in natural products like fruit and honey.

Vitamins are divided into groups: A, B, C, D and E. Vitamins keep our body healthy.

Minerals such as iron and calcium are also important for our health. Iron is important for our blood, and calcium for our teeth and bones.

It is important to get the right balance in your diet. You need to eat plenty of fruit and vegetables because they contain vitamins and minerals. You don't need to eat a large amount of protein, but you need to eat enough to keep your body strong.

You need to eat carbohydrates, but you don't need to eat a large quantity. Most people in their normal daily lives only need a little sugar and fat.

Use of English: Quantifiers with countable and uncountable nouns

Quantifiers tell you how many or how much there is of something.

Countable nouns are words like *book, student, egg*. They can be singular (*a book, a student, an egg*) or plural (*books, students, eggs*).

Uncountable nouns are words like *music, water, rice*. They are only singular.

quantifier	countable	quantifier	uncountable
a few a large / small number of several	vegetables, eggs, nuts	a little a large / small amount of	fruit, sugar, fat, ...

You can use *a lot of / lots of* and *plenty of* with both countable and uncountable nouns.

3 Use the phrases in the box to complete the sentences.

> a I have a few nuts or some fruit.
> b I like a little sugar.
> c I eat plenty of green vegetables.
> d I only eat a small amount of meat.
> e but she drinks several cups of tea every day.
> f I only eat a small number of vegetables.

1 In the summer, I eat lots of salads and in the winter *I eat plenty of green vegetables.*
2 My mum doesn't like coffee, _____ .
3 I don't like anything green, so _____ .
4 I'm not vegetarian, but _____ .
5 _____ in my tea.
6 I don't eat sweets, so if I'm hungry between meals, _____ .

Speaking

4 Do you have a balanced diet? Complete these sentences, so that they are true for you.

1 I eat plenty of … .
2 I only eat a small amount of … .
3 If I'm hungry between meals I have … .
4 I like a little (sugar / salt / pepper / oil) … in / on my … .
5 I like several kinds of (cereal / chocolate / fruit) … but my favourite is … .

5 Now talk with a partner about your diet.

A *I think I have a balanced diet. I eat fish and nuts and eggs so I get plenty of protein.*
B *What about carbohydrates?*
A *I eat a lot of rice and noodles because they give you energy.*
B *Do you eat a lot of sweet things?*
A *No, not really. What about you? Do you eat lots of fruit and vegetables?*

Be at your best!

- When do you feel your brain works best – first thing in the morning, just after lunch … ?

Reading

1 Read the leaflet. Who is it aimed at?

For your brain to work well, it needs …

… good food

Experts say that breakfast is much more important than any other meal. Your brain works better when you have eaten. So don't miss breakfast – especially before an exam! But you need to eat a good breakfast – junk food won't work.

… a regular supply of energy

Your brain needs a steady supply of energy, so you need to eat carbohydrates. They're found in bread, pasta, rice and pulses. Chocolate, biscuits and sweets are not good for your brain. They work more quickly than bread and rice, so they give you a short burst of energy, but afterwards you feel more tired.

… a constant supply of oxygen

Your brain needs oxygen, which it gets from exercise. Exercise improves your memory too. You also need a good supply of iron because iron helps your blood to carry oxygen round your body.

… water

Water is much better than sweet fizzy drinks. You need water because dehydration will stop your brain from working well. And remember, water isn't as expensive as fizzy drinks!

… a good night's sleep

Your brain needs several hours' sleep, so it can 'update' itself, just like a computer.

Experts say that when you revise for a test or an exam, you should get some sleep as quickly as possible after you've done your revision. This helps you to remember what you've learnt.

Vocabulary

2 What are these scientific words in your language?

1 brain   2 energy   3 oxygen   4 iron   5 blood   6 dehydration

3 Complete these sentences using the information in the text.

1 *You need to eat a healthy breakfast* because your brain performs better when you've eaten a good meal in the morning.
2 _____ because your brain needs a steady supply of energy.
3 _____ because they only give you a short burst of energy.
4 _____ because it helps your blood to carry oxygen round the body.
5 _____ because your brain doesn't work well if you're dehydrated.
6 _____ because your brain needs to process information.

Speaking

4 Use the sentences in Exercise 3 to ask and answer with a partner, like this:

A *Why do you need to eat a healthy breakfast?*   B   *Because …*

Listening 16

5 Listen to a nutritionist answering questions. What are the questions about?

6 Listen again. What does the nutritionist say about:

1 junk food?   **2** iron?   **3** sleep?

Use of English: Adjectives and adverbs; comparatives of adverbs

Adjectives describe people or things. They go before nouns: *a good breakfast.*

They can also go after some verbs, such as *be, feel, look*: *I feel tired.*

Adverbs tell us about a verb. They describe how an action is done. Remember that you can make an adverb by adding *-ly* to an adjective: clear – *clearly*, easy – *easily*, quick – *quickly*.

Speak clearly.   *I can do it easily.*   *Come quickly.*

However, some adverbs are irregular:

For your brain to work well, you need to eat breakfast.

To make comparisons using adverbs, use more + adverb (than) or as + adverb + as:

Chocolate, biscuits and sweets work more quickly than bread and rice.

You should get some sleep as quickly as possible after you've done your revision.

The comparatives of some adverbs are irregular:

adverb	comparative
well	better
badly	worse

---

7 Change the adjectives in brackets into the correct form of the adverb.

1 I do (*good*) in exams, but my brother does better.
   I do well in exams, but my brother does better.

2 I only sleep (*bad*) when I'm ill or anxious.

3 I don't study well in silence – I study (*good*) when I listen to music.

4 Chocolate gives you energy (*quick*) than bread, pasta or rice.

5 I play football badly when I haven't eaten enough, but I play (*bad*) when I've eaten too much!

6 I don't eat as (*quick*) as you. I enjoy my food!

Food and fitness

- What sort of food do you think long-distance runners need to eat? What should they drink? What else is important for them?

Reading

1 Read the article and answer the questions.

1 Which two things about the athletes surprised the writer?

2 Is there anything that surprises you about the athletes' diet and training programme?

Writing

2 Write questions for these answers.

Question	Answer
1 How often do the athletes eat?	Five times a day.
2 _____ ?	At 8 o'clock.
3 _____ ?	Bread, rice, potatoes, porridge, cabbage, beans and ugali.
4 _____ ?	Four times a week.
5 _____ ?	Yes, they drink a lot.
6 _____ ?	Twice a day, as a group.
7 _____ ?	At 5 o'clock.
8 _____ ?	10 to 15 kilometres in the morning and 6 to 8 kilometres in the afternoon.
9 _____ ?	Only a little.
10 _____ ?	About a litre a day.

Kenya's long-distance runners

Kenya's long-distance runners are among the best in the world. Is their diet and daily routine a key to the secret of their success? We spent a week at a training camp with ten top athletes to find out. This is what we discovered.

They eat five times a day:

08:00	Breakfast
10:00	Mid-morning snack
13:00	Lunch
16:00	Afternoon snack
19:00	Supper

The Kenyan runners' diet is based on bread, rice, potatoes, porridge, cabbage, beans and ugali (balls of cornmeal). Ugali is usually eaten with a sauce or vegetables.

Meat is eaten in fairly small amounts, just four times a week. The athletes drink a lot of tea with milk and sugar. They get all the vitamins and minerals they need from their food – they never take vitamin or mineral pills.

They usually train as a group twice a day. The first run is at 6 o'clock in the morning and the afternoon run is at 5 o'clock. They run 10 to 15 kilometres in the morning and 6 to 8 kilometres in the afternoon. Once a week, the two 1500-metre runners in the group run shorter distances at higher speeds.

An amazing aspect of the Kenyans' diet is the amount of food rich in carbohydrates that they eat. Every 24 hours, they have about 600 grams of carbohydrate to give them energy for their training. They only eat a little fat, most of it coming from the milk they have in their tea. Two-thirds of their protein comes from vegetables. They drink about a litre of water every day. Surprisingly, they drink more than a litre of tea every day, too. They always eat soon after training.

Rest and sleep are also an important part of the athletes' programme. They are always in bed early and they always get a good night's sleep.

Use of English: Position of adverbs of frequency

Adverbs of frequency tell you how often something happens.

Put adverbs such as *once a week* at the start or the end of a sentence:

Once a week, two of the runners run shorter distances.

They eat five times a day.

Put adverbs such as *always, usually, often, sometimes* and *never* with the verb:

after the verb *to be*

They are always in bed early.

before other verbs

They always get a good night's sleep.

How many times?

1 once
   NOT ~~one time~~
2 twice
   NOT ~~two times~~
3 three times
4 four times

3 Complete these sentences with adverbs of frequency. Look back at the text to help you.

1 The athletes usually train as a group *twice a day*.
2 Meat is eaten _____ .
3 Ugali is _____ eaten with a sauce or vegetables.
4 The athletes _____ take vitamin or mineral pills.
5 They run 6 to 8 kilometres _____ .
6 _____ they have about 600 grams of carbohydrate.
7 They drink about a litre of water _____ .
8 They _____ eat soon after training.

Did you know?

In Kenya, porridge is made from cornmeal and other cereals cooked with water. It's served hot, with milk or butter, salt or sugar. Do you have anything in your country that's similar to porridge?

4 Ask and answer the questions with a partner. Try to use adverbs of frequency in your answers.

1 What do you have for breakfast? *I usually have … but at the weekend I often have …*
2 What do you drink with breakfast?
3 Do you ever have a snack between meals? What do you have?
4 How often do you do sport or exercise?
5 Do you do anything special at the weekend?
6 How many hours' sleep do you have each night?

Project: Plan a menu

5 Work in groups. Imagine you're going to have a perfectly balanced diet tomorrow. What are you going to eat for each meal? Plan a menu.

Menu

Breakfast

Mid-morning snack

Lunch

Afternoon snack

Supper

a

- **Topics** Animal groups; inherited characteristics; the world of the polar bear and habitat shift
- **Use of English** *so am I, so do I*; relative clauses with *which* as a subject pronoun

The world of animals

b

- Think of your favourite animal. Describe it without saying what it is. Ask other members of the class to guess what it is.

Reading

1 Read about the animals and match the descriptions to the pictures. Say what each animal is: a bird, a mammal, a fish, an amphibian or a reptile.

1 The roadrunner lives on land and doesn't often fly. It has very strong legs and can run at speeds of up to 32 kilometres per hour. It has a very sharp beak. It can kill a snake with one bite.

2 The green tree frog has sticky toes, so it can hang on smooth leaves and branches. It's so small and light that a leaf can take its weight.

3 The sloth moves very slowly. It can't run away from other animals, so it hides. It hangs upside down under the branches of trees, so that it can't be seen. The sloth's fur grows down from its stomach to its back, so that the rain runs off more easily.

4 Many people think chameleons change colour, so that they can't be seen by other animals. But scientists disagree. Their studies show that light, temperature and mood cause chameleons to change colour. Chameleons also change colour to help them communicate with other chameleons. Their eyes can move through a full 360-degree circle, so that they can see all around them. The name *chameleon* comes from the Greek words *chamai* (on the earth) and *leon* (lion).

5 The Siamese fighting fish are known for their brilliant colours and their large fins. It's the male fish which looks after the young fish, not the female. As their name suggests, they fight, sometimes until one of them dies.

Listening 17

2 Listen and follow the information about the animals in Exercise 1. There is one piece of additional information about each animal. What is it?

Vocabulary

3 Complete the description of each animal group with one of the following sentences:

a They live mainly on land, but breed in water.
b Most take in oxygen from the water through gills; a few also have lungs.
c They have feathers and most of them can fly.
d Most live on land and most lay their eggs on land too.
e They produce milk to feed their babies.

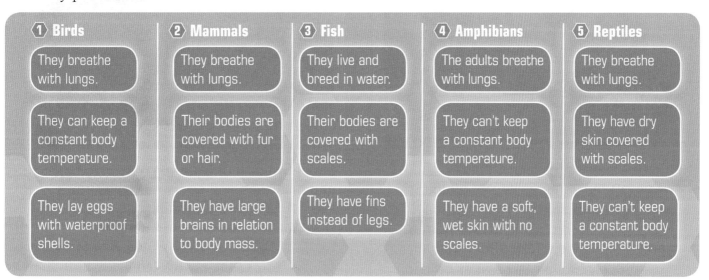

① Birds	② Mammals	③ Fish	④ Amphibians	⑤ Reptiles
They breathe with lungs.	They breathe with lungs.	They live and breed in water.	The adults breathe with lungs.	They breathe with lungs.
They can keep a constant body temperature.	Their bodies are covered with fur or hair.	Their bodies are covered with scales.	They can't keep a constant body temperature.	They have dry skin covered with scales.
They lay eggs with waterproof shells.	They have large brains in relation to body mass.	They have fins instead of legs.	They have a soft, wet skin with no scales.	They can't keep a constant body temperature.

4 Match the words to the definitions.

1	to breathe	**a**	the surface of an animal's body
2	lungs	**b**	small, flat pieces of skin on a fish or snake
3	shell	**c**	soft hair that covers the bodies of some animals
4	feathers	**d**	the hard outer cover of an egg
5	fur	**e**	they allow a fish to breathe
6	to breed	**f**	they cover a bird's skin and they keep it warm
7	scales	**g**	they're inside your body and they fill with air when you breathe
8	fins	**h**	the thin flat parts of fish that help it to swim
9	gills	**i**	to take air into your body and let it out again
10	skin	**j**	to produce babies

Writing and speaking

5 Write three questions about the animals in the photos.

Which animal … ?, Where … ?, Why … ?, How … ?, What … ?

Ask other members of the class your questions.

Who are you like?

- Look at the photos of the two families. Describe the people in each family. Who do the children look like, their mother or their father?

I think I look like my mum. People say we've got the same smile. My brother is younger than me. _____¹. My hair is wavy like my brother's, but his hair is darker than mine. I take after my mum. _____². My brother takes after my dad. _____³.

I'm of Swedish origin. I've got blonde hair and blue eyes and so have the children. I've got straight hair and so has Amelia. However, Jessica has got wavy hair. _____⁴. She's very easy-going and so is he. _____⁵. She's quite independent and so am I.

Reading

1 Read the texts and put these sentences in the correct places.

- Amelia takes after me.
- He's like my dad.
- I like music and so does she.
- She's more like her father.
- They're both crazy about football.

2 Read the texts again. Who is talking in each photo?

3 Find words in the text to describe

- hair colour and shade
- type of hair
- personality.

Use of English: *so am I; so do I*

To say that people are the same, or do the same things, we can use *so* + verb + pronoun or noun:
I've got straight hair and so has she.
She's quite independent and so am I.

When the verb is a main verb, we need to use *do, does, did* after *so*:
I love music and so does she.

Note the order of the words:
so have I.   NOT   ~~so I have.~~
so am I.   NOT   ~~so I am.~~
so does she.   NOT   ~~so she does.~~

Language tip

Note the differences between *to look like, to be like* and *to take after.*

physical similarities
to look like
I look like my mum. We've both got brown hair and blue eyes.

physical / personality similarities
to be like
I'm like my older brother. We've both got dark curly hair and we're easy-going.

to take after
I take after my dad. I'm quite tall and I'm quite quiet.

4 Join the sentences using *and so*.

1 I've got brown hair. My mum's also got brown hair.
I've got brown hair and so has my mum.
2 I like football. My dad likes football too.
3 My dad's got short hair. My brother's got short hair too.
4 I like music. My mum also likes music.
5 My daughters have got brown eyes. My husband has also got brown eyes.
6 My older daughter is easy-going. My husband is also easy-going.

Speaking

5 Work with a partner. Ask and answer these questions.

1 Who are you like in your family?
2 Who do you take after?

Try to use these sentences in your answers:

- So am I.
- So have I.
- So do I.
- So is he / she.
- So has he / she.
- So does he / she.

6 Work in small groups. Discuss these questions.

- What are you interested in?
- What are you good at?
- Do you think you've inherited your interests and abilities from your parents, or have they come from your environment?

Animals on the move

- In which countries do you find polar bears? Can they swim? What do they eat?

Reading

1 Look at the title of the magazine article and the photo at the bottom of this page. What does the word 'shrinking' mean?

2 Read the article. Why is the polar bear's world shrinking?

Vocabulary

3 Look at the Fact file and find:

1 A word which means 'meat-eating'.
2 Three types of marine mammal.
3 A word for the feet of certain types of animal like bears, cats and rabbits.
4 An adjective to describe skin between an animal's toes.
5 A word for a baby bear.

4 Find words in the article to complete these sentences.

1 When ice _____ it turns to water.
2 Wild animals have to _____ for their food.
3 When people or animals have no food for a long time, they _____ .
4 Polar bears are moving from the ice to the land. They're _____ their habitat.
5 Animals are in danger due to climate change. We need to help them to _____ .

THE SHRINKING WORLD OF
THE POLAR BEAR

Polar bears live in the Arctic, which is one of the planet's coldest environments. They move around on the Arctic ice sheets and swim in the coastal waters. They feed mainly on seals, which they catch with their huge paws when the seals are resting on the ice or coming up to breathe. However, global warming is changing their way of life.

Climate change is a problem for the bears. As the sea ice melts, they can't move around and hunt so freely. They get very hungry and begin to starve. They're actually very good at starving for a time – they can starve for several months. But eventually they need to eat. This is why they're shifting their habitat. They're spending more time on land and less on the ice. They're going into towns and villages and looking for food in rubbish bins. They're not afraid of people and may attack them when they're very hungry.

Polar bears can't live with people, but their natural habitat is disappearing. How will they survive?

POLAR BEAR FACT FILE

TYPE: mammal
HABITAT: the Arctic regions of Russia, Alaska, Canada, Greenland and Norway
DIET: carnivorous (seals, walruses, whales)
AVERAGE LIFE SPAN: 25 to 30 years

- Polar bears have large webbed front paws, which help them to swim.
- They have a thick coat of fur, which covers a layer of fat.
- On the bottom of their paws they have fur, which protects them against the cold and helps them to walk on ice.
- Under their fur the bears have black skin, which helps them to get as much heat as possible from the sun.
- Females usually have two cubs, which live with their mother for over two years.
- The females look after the cubs with no help from the males. In fact, male polar bears will sometimes kill the young cubs.

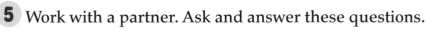

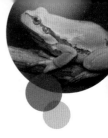

5 Work with a partner. Ask and answer these questions.

Student A

1 What type of animal is a polar bear?
It's a mammal.
2 Where does it live?
3 What does it eat?
4 How long does it live?
5 Why do polar bears have fur on the bottom of their paws?
6 How long do young polar bears stay with their mother?

Student B

1 How do polar bears catch seals?
2 Why is the sea ice melting?
3 Why is it becoming harder for bears to hunt in the Arctic?
4 Why are polar bears going into towns and villages?
5 What do they find to eat in towns and villages?
6 Why are polar bears dangerous to people?

Use of English: Relative clauses with *which* as a subject pronoun

Notice how you can join these two sentences by using *which* to replace *it* or *they*:

Polar bears live in the Arctic. It is one of the planet's coldest environments.
Polar bears live in the Arctic, which is one of the planet's coldest environments.

Polar bears have large webbed front paws. They help them to swim.
Polar bears have large webbed front paws, which help them to swim.

What happens to the words *it* and *they* when you use *which*?

---

6 Use *which* to join these sentences together.

1 They have a thick coat of fur. It covers a layer of fat.
   They have a thick coat of fur, which covers a layer of fat.
2 On the bottom of their paws they have fur. It protects them against the cold and helps them to walk on the ice.
3 Under their fur, the bears have black skin. It helps them to get as much heat as possible from the sun.
4 Females usually have two cubs. They live with their mother for over two years.
5 They feed mainly on seals. They are easy to catch when they are resting on the ice.

Project: Bears in the wild

7 Write a fact file on another kind of bear, like the one about the polar bear.

- the grizzly bear
- the giant panda
- the black bear
- the brown bear
- the spectacled bear
- the sloth bear
- the sun bear

Fiction

1 **Answer the questions.**

1 Do you think there is a special bond (link, connection) between people and horses? Why?

2 Why did people value horses in the past? Why do they value them now?

War Horse, by Michael Morpurgo, is the story of a horse called Joey. He becomes separated from the boy who owns him when he is sold to the cavalry in the First World War. Joey's experience of the war is at the heart of the book, which has been made into a play and a film.

2 Read the extract from *War Horse*. Who is the narrator (the 'I')? Who is Albert? Who is Joey? Who is Zoey?

3 **Answer the questions.**

1 How does Albert create 'a bond of trust and affection' with Joey?

2 Does the writer focus more on appearance or feelings?

3 How are Albert and his father different?

4 How does Joey's attitude to Albert change?

4 **Answer these questions about the vocabulary and style of the extract.**

1 In the first three paragraphs, which words and phrases create a positive, calm and quiet atmosphere?

2 How many verbs to do with the sense of touch can you find?

3 Why does the writer include direct speech (the actual words people used)? Could he have created the same effect if he had only used narrative description?

5 Animals often feature in stories, poems, films and songs for children. Why do you think this is?

A scene from the play *War Horse*

Albert was about the same height as me
and talked so gently as he approached that I was
immediately calmed and not a little intrigued, and so
stood where I was against the wall. I jumped at first
5 when he touched me, but could see at once that he
meant me no harm. He smoothed my back first and
then my neck, talking all the while about what a fine
time we would have together, how I would grow up
to be the smartest horse in the whole wide world, and
10 how we would go out hunting together.

After a bit he began to rub me gently with his coat.
He rubbed me until I was dry and then dabbed salted
water onto my face where the skin had been rubbed
raw. He brought in some sweet hay and a bucket of
15 cool, deep water. I do not believe he stopped talking all
the time. As he turned to go out of the stable I called
out to him to thank him and he seemed to understand
for he smiled broadly and stroked my nose.

"We'll get along, you and I", he said kindly. "I shall
20 call you Joey, only because it rhymes with Zoey, and
then maybe, yes maybe because it suits you. I'll be out
again in the morning – and don't worry, I'll look after
you. I promise you that. Sweet dreams, Joey. "

"You should never talk to horses, Albert, " said his
25 mother from outside. "They never understand you.
They're stupid creatures. Obstinate and stupid, that's
what your father says, and he's known horses all his
life."

"Father just doesn't understand them, " said
30 Albert. "I think he's frightened of them. "

I went over to the door and watched Albert and
his mother walking away and up into the darkness. I
knew then that I had found a friend for life, that there
was an instinctive and immediate bond of trust and
35 affection between us. Next to me old Zoey leant over
her door to try to touch me, but our noses would not
quite meet.

War Horse by Michael Morpurgo, Egmont Press, 2006

3   **intrigued** very interested
5–6 **he meant me no harm** he wasn't going to
hurt me
6   **to smooth** to move your hand across
something to make it flat
11 **to rub** to press and move your hand, a cloth
or an object over a surface
12 **to dab** to touch something gently several
times with a cloth
14 **raw** skin that is red and painful because it has
been rubbed too much
14 **hay** dry grass
14 **bucket** a large container for carrying water
16 **stable** a place to keep horses
18 **to smile broadly** to give a big smile
18 **to stroke** to gently smooth the fur of an
animal
19 **to get along** to get on well
21 **it suits you** it's right for you
26 **obstinate** not willing to change your ideas
34 **instinctive** natural
34 **bond of trust** an understanding that each
will always be true to the other

Review of Units 7–8

Vocabulary

Food and health

1 Give an example of food which contains …

1 protein
2 carbohydrate
3 fat
4 sugar

2 What are these scientific words?

1 It's in your head and you need it to help you think.
2 It's red and it carries oxygen round your body.
3 The chemical symbol for this is O and you find it in air and water.
4 If you don't drink enough water there's a danger of this.
5 You need food to give you this.
6 It's a mineral and it helps to take oxygen round your body.

The world of animals

3 Complete the characteristics of the different animal groups.

1 Birds
They lay eggs with waterproof shells[1].
Most of them can fly.
Their skin is covered with _____[2] to keep them warm.

2 Mammals
Their bodies are covered with hair or _____[3].
They have large brains.
They produce _____[4] to feed their babies.

3 Fish
They live and breed in water.
Their bodies are covered with _____[5]
Most take in oxygen from the water through _____[6]; a few also have lungs.

4 Amphibians
The adults breathe with _____[7].
They have a soft, wet skin with no scales.
They live mainly on land, but breed in _____[8].

5 Reptiles
They breathe with lungs.
They have dry skin covered with _____[9].
Most live on land and most lay their _____[10] on land too.

Use of English

4 Choose the correct option for each sentence.

1 Do you eat _____ fruit?
   a many
   b a large number of
   c a lot of
2 You only need _____ salt.
   a a little
   b several
   c a few
3 I don't eat meat, but I get _____ protein.
   a much
   b plenty of
   c plenty
4 I don't have many snacks, but I sometimes eat _____ nuts.
   a a little
   b few
   c a few
5 I like bananas and apples, but I don't eat _____ fruit.
   a a large number of
   b a large amount of
   c many
6 Avocado pears are good for you because they contain _____ vitamins and minerals.
   a a little
   b several
   c plenty

5 Put the adverb of frequency in the correct place in the sentence.

1 Polar bears *usually* eat seals. (*usually*)
2 Polar bears swim long distances to find food. (*sometimes*)
3 Polar bears have two cubs. (*usually*)
4 The cubs live with their mother until they are at least two years old. (*always*)
5 Polar bear cubs play together. (*often*)
6 Polar bears are dangerous to humans when they're hungry. (*sometimes*)
7 The male polar bear stays with the cubs to look after them. (*never*)
8 Adult female polar bears give birth. (*once every two or three years*)
9 When the cubs are very young, the mother feeds them. (*up to six times a day*)
10 The cubs are born with their eyes closed. (*always*)

6 Join the sentences using *and so*.

1 Mammals breathe with lungs. Birds and reptiles also breathe with lungs.
   Mammals breathe with lungs and so do birds and reptiles.
2 Birds lay eggs. Most reptiles lay eggs.
3 Mammals can keep a constant body temperature. Birds can keep a constant body temperature too.
4 Fish breed in water. Amphibians breed in water too.
5 Polar bears have lost some of their natural habitat. Elephants have also lost some of their natural habitat.

7 Match the sentences and join them using *which*.

   1e Our bodies need protein, which can be found in meat, fish, eggs and pulses.
1 Our bodies need protein.
2 We all need calcium.
3 You need to eat some carbohydrates.

4 Meat, some vegetables and pulses contain iron.
5 You should eat plenty of fruit and vegetables.

a It makes our teeth and bones stronger.
b They give you the energy you need, especially if you're doing a lot of exercise.
c They give you a lot of the vitamins and minerals you need.
d It's important for your blood because it helps it to carry oxygen round the body.
e It can be found in meat, fish, eggs and pulses.

General knowledge quiz

8 Answer the questions.

1 They are divided into groups, A, B, C, D and E, for example, and they keep our bodies healthy. What are they?
2 What is the word for the condition which is a result of not drinking enough water?
3 Polar bears are carnivorous. What does this mean?
4 Which two animal groups have scales?
5 They live mainly on land, but breed in water. Which animal group is it?
6 What kind of animal is a roadrunner? And what is unusual about it?
7 Look at the picture. What is it? And what does its name mean?
8 In which part of the world do sloths live?
9 What colour is the skin of a polar bear?
10 Where do polar bears live?

9 World records

- **Topics** The ancient Olympics; the Paralympics; world records; a profile of an athlete
- **Use of English** Past perfect; pronouns *everyone*, *anyone*, *no one*; comparatives and superlatives of adverbs

The ancient Olympics

- Do you know anything about the origin of the Olympic Games?

Reading

1 Read about the ancient Olympics on page 73. Find three things you didn't already know.

2 Answer the questions.
1 Where and when did the first Olympics take place?
2 What was a *stadion*?
3 What was there at the beginning and end of the five-day Olympics?
4 How many sports were there in the pentathlon and what were they?
5 'Winning was everything.' Why?
6 Did women take part in sport in ancient Greece? How do you know?
7 How did people get to Olympia?
8 What did Olympic champions wear on their head?

Use of English: Past perfect

We use the past perfect when we're already talking about something in the past and we want to talk about something that happened before that.

| had | + | past participle |

Some had walked for several days to get there.

Affirmative	*By the time the Games started, 40,000 spectators had arrived in Olympia to watch them.*
Negative	*The Games hadn't taken place for over a thousand years.*
Question	*How far had they come?*

---

3 Write these sentences. One verb has to go in the past simple and the other has to go in the past perfect.
1 She (*feel*) tired because she (*not eat*) anything before the race.
   She felt tired because she hadn't eaten anything before the race.
2 The race (*finish*) by the time we (*arrive*) at the stadium.
3 He (*not take part*) in the race because he (*not do*) enough training.
4 He (*not win*) the chariot race because a wheel (*come off*) halfway round the track.
5 (*he / win*) a race before (*he / compete*) in this year's Games?

Speaking

4 Work in groups. Discuss this question: What are the similarities and differences between the ancient Olympics and the modern Olympics? Think about:
- how often
- where
- sports and events
- the competitors
- the prizes
- the spectators.

The modern Olympic Games began in 1896. They were based on the ancient Olympic Games, which hadn't taken place for over a thousand years before that.

The ancient Olympics began in 776 BCE in Olympia in Greece and they took place there every four years until 394 CE. The first Games were a one-day event and had just one running race, the *stadion*, a short sprint of between 180 and 240 metres – the length of the stadium. The first ever Olympic race was won by a cook called Koroibos.

The Games were popular and, in about 400 BCE, they were extended to five days, with an opening and a closing ceremony. At the end of the second day, the pentathlon took place: discus, javelin and long jump, followed by running and finally wrestling. There were also boxing matches, chariot races and horse races.

When the athletes arrived to compete in the Games, they had trained in the gymnasium for at least ten months. There were no medals, no prizes and no second or third places. Winning was everything. However, back in his home city, the winner received money and vats of olive oil; he got the best seats at the theatre; and he probably never worked again.

Women didn't take part in the ancient Olympics, but they had their own women-only Games, which took place every four years.

By the time the Games started, 40,000 spectators had arrived in Olympia to watch them. How far had they come? Some had walked for several days; others had come by sea from places as far away as Spain, Italy and Egypt.

On the final day of the Games, the champions were crowned with olive wreaths and there was a feast for all the competitors.

The Paralympics

- Look at the photo. What sort of race do you think it is?

Reading

1 Read what some people said about the Paralympics. How do they feel?

'Everything about the Paralympics is brilliant. The athletes are amazing. When Alan Oliveira won, everyone in the stadium cheered. Lots of people jumped up from their seats and a few were in tears.'

'Is there anyone who wasn't inspired by what they saw?'

'The sound in the stadium was incredible. I've never heard anything like it.'

'These athletes are an inspiration. Nothing stops them. They make you think no one should ever give up.'

'The Paralympics are more exciting than the Olympics. Anyone who has seen the blade runners will tell you that.'

'Everyone is going to be talking about it at school. Everybody is going to be saying, 'We were there, we saw him break the world record!''

Did you know?

The first Paralympics (Olympic Games for disabled people) took place in Rome in 1960. There were about 400 athletes from 23 countries. The word 'Paralympics' comes from the Greek *para* meaning 'beside' plus 'Olympics'. Can you name a paralympic sport?

Listening 18

2 Before you listen, look again at the photo and answer these questions.

1 The athelete in the photo is Alan Oliveira. When he was a very young child he had both legs amputated below the knee. What do you think 'amputate' means?

2 He began to use carbon fibre blades at the age of fifteen. What are carbon fibre blades?

3 Listen to this feature on Alan Oliveira. What do you think his attitude to his disability is?

4 Listen again and complete the summary. You can listen more than once.

SUMMARY
Alan Oliveira
1 By the age of two, he had learned _____ .
2 By the age of four, _____ .
3 At the age of eight, _____ .
   He knew then that _____ .
4 At school, he started _____ .
   He could run _____ .
5 At the age of thirteen, _____ .
6 At the age of fifteen, _____ .
7 In 2008, _____ .
8 In 2012, _____ .

Speaking

5 Work with a partner.
Student A: Ask Student B questions based on 1 to 4 in the summary in Exercise 4.

Student B: Ask Student A questions based on 5 to 8 in the summary in Exercise 4.

1 *How old was Alan Oliveira when he learned to walk?*
2 *What could he do by the time he was four?*

5 *What happened when he was thirteen?*
6 *When did he start using carbon fibre blades?*

Use of English: Pronouns *everyone, anyone, no one; everything, anything, nothing*

After these pronouns, we use singular verbs.

Everyone is going to be talking about it at school. *Is there anyone who wasn't inspired by what they saw?* *No one should ever give up.*	everyone is the same as *everybody* anyone is the same as *anybody* no one is the same as *nobody*
Everything is brilliant. The sound in the stadium was incredible. I've never heard anything like it. *Nothing stops these athletes.*	We usually use *anyone* and *anything* with negatives and questions. However, there is a special use of *anyone* and *anything* to mean 'it doesn't matter who / what': *The Paralympics are more exciting than the Olympics. Anyone who has seen the blade runners will tell you that. Anything can happen!*

---

6 Complete each sentence about the Paralympics with a word from the box.

> everybody   everything   anybody
> anything   nobody   nothing

1 There were lots of events going on at the same time, but *everything* was very well organised.
2 The opening ceremony was brilliant. I've never seen _____ like it.
3 It was a fantastic event. _____ was really happy to be there.
4 We all got tickets, so _____ was disappointed.
5 A lot of people bought souvenirs like T-shirts and baseball caps. At the end of the evening, there was _____ left.
6 I was amazed that _____ could go so fast in a wheelchair.

Writing

7 Think of a sporting event you've enjoyed at school, on TV or in a stadium. Write your impressions of the event.

I've never seen anything like it!
It was brilliant / exciting / amazing / fantastic …
Everybody / Nobody was …
Everything / Nothing …
When …, everybody cheered / stood up

Higher, faster, further

- Do you know any world record holders?

Reading and speaking

1 Work on the World Records Quiz in small teams.

- Organise your team. Start like this:

  We need a team name. What shall we call ourselves?

  Who's going to read out the questions?

  Who's going to be team captain, to decide on the correct answers?

  Who's going to write down the answers?

- You will need a sheet of paper for your answer sheet. Write your team name at the top of it.

Listening 19

2 Listen and check the answers.

WORLD RECORDS QUIZ

SPORT

1 Which two countries have done best in the men's modern pentathlon since it was introduced at the modern Olympic Games?

   a China   d Russia
   b Poland   e Hungary
   c Sweden

2 What can athletes throw furthest?

   a the discus   c the javelin
   b the shot put

3 Women have thrown the discus further in the Olympics than men. Why is this?

   a Women are better at throwing than men.
   b The women's discus is bigger than the men's discus.
   c The men's discus is twice as heavy as the women's discus.

Use of English: Comparatives and superlatives of adverbs

We normally use *more* and *most* to make comparative and superlative adverbs.

You can run the 400 metres more quickly than I can run the 200 metres.
The most quickly I've run 100 metres is 12.9 seconds. It's my personal best.

The following comparatives and superlatives are irregular:

adverb	comparative	superlative
well	better	(the) best
badly	worse	(the) worst
far	further	(the) furthest
much	more	(the) most

Some comparatives and superlatives of adverbs end in -er and -est:

adverb	comparative	superlative
fast	faster	fastest
long	longer	longest
high	higher	highest

You can make negatives like this:
Sound does not travel as quickly as light.

NATURAL WORLD

4 Which animal sleeps the most?
a a sloth   c a koala
b a giraffe   d a tiger

5 Which animal runs fastest over a short distance?
a a lion   b a cheetah   c a leopard

6 Which animal weighs the most?
a an African elephant
b a blue whale
c a hippopotamus

7 Which animal lives longest?
a the killer whale   c the condor
b the giant tortoise

SCIENCE, TECHNOLOGY AND COMMUNICATION

8 Which of these is true?
a Light travels more slowly through air than through water.
b Sound doesn't travel as quickly as light.
c An Olympic sprinter runs faster than the speed of sound.

9 Which bridge takes longest to cross?
a the Jiaozhou Bay Bridge in eastern China
b the Lake Pontchartrain Bridge in Louisiana in the USA
c the Sydney Harbour Bridge in Australia

10 In 2010, a paper plane flew higher than any paper plane had flown before. How high did it fly? (Clue: It was launched by a large helium balloon!)
a 500m   b 2km   c 27.4km

3 Complete the sentences with the correct comparative or superlative adverb.

1 Sweden and Hungary have done *best* in the men's modern pentathlon.
2 Athletes can throw the javelin _____ than the discus or the shot put.
3 Of all the animals, the koala sleeps the _____. It sleeps _____ than the sloth.
4 Cheetahs run _____ than lions or leopards. Leopards don't run _____ as lions or cheetahs.
5 The animal that weighs _____ is the blue whale. It weighs much _____ than an elephant or a hippopotamus.
6 Giant tortoises live _____ than killer whales or condors.

Project: Write a biography

4 Which athlete do you most admire? Write a short biography for an Internet sports magazine. Illustrate your biography with photos if possible.

He / She was born in …
At school he / she was good at …
When he / she was (16), he / she …
In 20 … he / she won …
Recently he / she has …

5 Use your biography to give a presentation to the class.

10 Parts and percentages

- **Topics** The language of Maths; the golden ratio; a class survey
- **Use of English** The definite article with places and buildings; expressions of quantity followed by *of*

Talking numbers

- Are you good at Maths? Which aspects of Maths do you find easy or difficult?

Vocabulary

1 Work in pairs. Answer the questions in the *Numbers quiz*. Write down the answers.

2 Write the following as symbols:

1	add +	3	subtract	5	multiply
2	plus	4	minus	6	divide

3 Write these sums using numerals and symbols.

Example: twelve times two 12×2

1 a quarter plus an eighth
2 four fifths minus three fifths
3 five plus fifty-five
4 ten per cent of fifty
5 six multiplied by sixteen
6 twenty divided by four
7 fourteen take away five
8 one point two five plus two point two five
9 six into thirty-six
10 half of twenty-two

4 Add up your scores.

Exercise 1:   / 15
Exercise 2:   / 5
Exercise 3:   / 20 *(two points for each answer)*

Marks out of 40:

For an extra ten points, solve the sums in Exercise 3.
Exercise 3 answers: / 10

FINAL SCORE: / 50

Show your final score as a percentage.

Listening 20

5 Listen to the number games. Follow the instructions.

Speaking

6 Work in pairs on these maths puzzles.

Student A: Give these instructions to your partner.

n?   *Think of a number.*
× 2   *Double it. / Multiply it by two.*
+ 9
− 3
÷ 2
– the original number
Answer?   (The answer is three.)

Student B: Give these instructions to your partner.

n?
× 3
+ 45
× 2
÷ 6
– the original number
Answer?   (The answer is fifteen.)

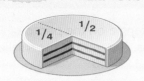

Numbers quiz

1 How much of the cake has been eaten?
   a a quarter   b a third   c a half

2 How much of the cake is left?
   a two thirds   b two fifths   c three quarters

3 What percentage of the cake has been eaten?
   a thirty per cent
   b twenty-five per cent
   c fifteen per cent

4 What percentage of the cake is left?
   a sixty per cent
   b seventy per cent
   c seventy-five per cent

5 If the full price is £15, how do you work out the cost of this item?
   a You multiply fifteen by two.
   b You divide fifteen by two.
   c You subtract five from fifteen.

6 In Maths, which two words mean the same as 'take away'?
   a subtract   b minus   c plus

7 You have to run five times round a 400-metre running track. How do you work out how far you've run?
   a 400 ÷ 5   b 400 x 5   c $\frac{400}{5}$

8 There are 50,000 spectators in the football stadium. Ninety per cent are home fans. How do you work out how many home fans there are in the stadium?
   a 50,000 x 90% = 45,000
   b 50,000 – 9000 = 41,000
   c 50,000 – 90% = 5000

9 Add 0.25 to 0.5. What's the answer?
   a zero point five five
   b zero point seven
   c zero point seven five

10 Add the two fractions in the picture. What is the total?
   a one and a quarter
   b three quarters
   c three eighths

11 Now multiply the two fractions in the picture above. What is the answer?
   a one sixth   b one eighth
   c six eighths

12 The answer is seven. What is the question?
   a What's eighteen minus twelve?
   b What's three into twenty-one?
   c What's two point five plus three point five?

13 If you double the amount of water you drink in a day you drink ...
   a half as much   b twice as much
   c fifty per cent less

14 If you double an odd number you ...
   a always get an odd number
   b always get an even number
   c sometimes get an odd number and sometimes get an even number

15 If you got ninety per cent in your last test, how many marks did you get?
   a nineteen out of twenty
   b eleven out of twenty
   c eighteen out of twenty

   90% Well done!

Did you know?

Countries have different ways of using commas and full stops in long numbers and decimals.

In the UK, this is how people use commas and full stops:

10,000	ten thousand
1,000,000	a million
2.75	two point seven five

€25,456.68 twenty-five thousand, four hundred and fifty-six euros, sixty-eight

In your country, where do you put the commas and full stops in these numbers?

Places and proportions

- If there are 20 teachers and 300 students, the ratio of teachers to students is 20 : 300. You can simplify this ratio as 2 : 30 or 1 : 15. The ratio of teachers to students is 1 : 15.

- How many teachers are there at your school? How many students are there? What is the ratio of teachers to students?

Reading

1 Look at the pictures, read the text and answer these questions.

1 Which of these shapes can you see in the photos?

pyramid	rectangle	square
triangle	circle	

2 What is the mathematical name for the ratio 1 : 1.618?

3 Why have architects and artists used this ratio in their work?

2 Find out how the golden ratio works. Follow these instructions.

Look at the big rectangle on the photo of The Parthenon in Athens. The ratio of the smaller side to the larger side is 1 : 1.618.

The Parthenon, Athens, Greece

Now look at the diagram next to the photo of The Great Pyramid at Giza, one of the Seven Wonders of the Ancient World. The ratio of ab to ac is 1 : 1.618. This is known as the golden ratio.

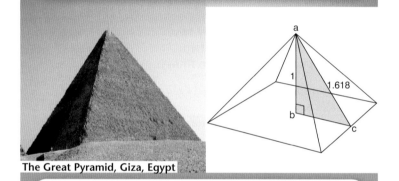

The Great Pyramid, Giza, Egypt

1 : 1.618 is called the golden ratio for two reasons. The first is that it's pleasing to the eye; the second is that it produces a perfect mathematical proportion. The golden ratio has been used by many architects and artists in their work.

1 Take a piece of paper. Draw a rectangle. The length of the sides must be 10cm by 16.18cm – that is, in the ratio 1 : 1.618.

2 Cut a square from the rectangle using the shorter side of the rectangle as one side of the square.

3 The rectangle that remains is in the same proportion as the original rectangle, that is 1 : 1.618.

4 You can now repeat steps 2 and 3. Again you will get a rectangle in the proportion of 1 : 1.618.

Speaking

3 Work with a partner. Answer these questions.

1 How many rectangular objects can you think of which have the approximate proportions of the golden ratio?

2 Which of these people use ratios in their work or daily life? How do they use them?

Town planners use ratios when they're working out the right balance between people, buildings, open spaces and roads.

town planners	architects
chefs	chemists
dieticians	engineers
farmers	painters
tourists	

designing a building

mixing medicines

mixing colours

building a bridge

planning a balanced diet

mixing food ingredients

working out relative values of currencies

mixing food for animals

Use of English: The definite article with places and buildings

We use *the* before some places and buildings, but not with others. Here is a guide.

With *the*

famous buildings: *the* Parthenon, *the* Great Pyramid

oceans, seas, rivers: *the* Pacific

most geographical regions: *the* north, *the* central plateau, *the* Antarctic

mountain ranges and island groups: *the* Andes, *the* Maldives

Without *the*

continents and most countries: Asia, Egypt

lakes and most mountains: Lake Titicaca, Everest

place name + building: Athens airport, Mumbai Central Station

Use *the* with

plural names of countries: *the* United Arab Emirates, *the* Netherlands, *the* United States

names which include *republic*, *kingdom*: *the* Czech Republic, *the* United Kingdom

Writing and speaking

4 Work in pairs. Write down an example of each of the following.

1 a continent
2 a country
3 a famous building
4 a group of islands
5 a lake
6 a mountain
7 a mountain range
8 a river

5 Work with another pair. See if they can guess the places you wrote down in Exercise 4. Give them clues:

It's a continent./ It's a country in … The capital city is …/ It's a famous building in …/ It's a group of islands near …/ It's a lake in …/ It's a mountain in …/ It's a mountain range in …/ It's a river in …

Most of us use the Internet

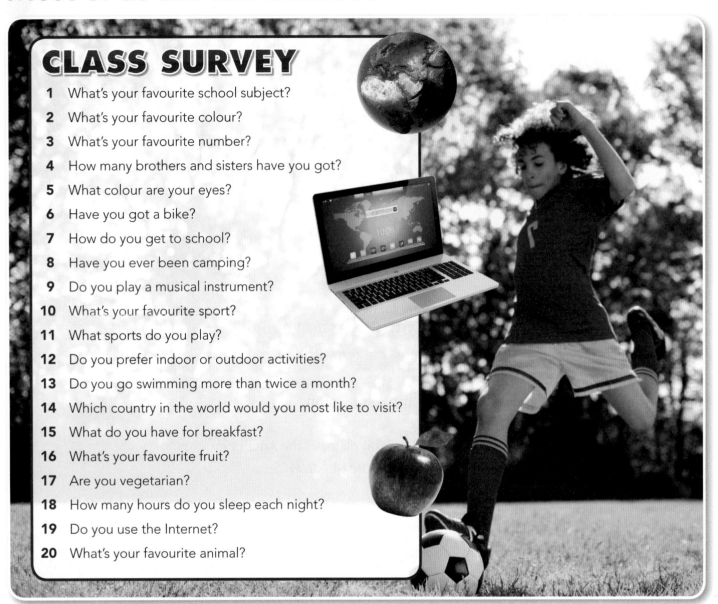

CLASS SURVEY

1 What's your favourite school subject?
2 What's your favourite colour?
3 What's your favourite number?
4 How many brothers and sisters have you got?
5 What colour are your eyes?
6 Have you got a bike?
7 How do you get to school?
8 Have you ever been camping?
9 Do you play a musical instrument?
10 What's your favourite sport?
11 What sports do you play?
12 Do you prefer indoor or outdoor activities?
13 Do you go swimming more than twice a month?
14 Which country in the world would you most like to visit?
15 What do you have for breakfast?
16 What's your favourite fruit?
17 Are you vegetarian?
18 How many hours do you sleep each night?
19 Do you use the Internet?
20 What's your favourite animal?

Reading and speaking

1 **Do the class survey.**

Question number	Alicia	Javed	Anjuma
1			
2			
3			

- Work in groups of four or five.
- Make a chart like this and write your names at the top. Do the survey and record your answers.
- Share your information with the rest of the class. For each of the questions in the survey, note down how many students in the class chose the most popular option. For example, if 9 out of 25 students voted for Maths, write: Question 1: *Maths 9 / 25*. Convert the answers to percentages, like this:

$$\frac{9 \times 100}{25} = 36\%$$

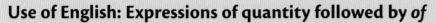

Use of English: Expressions of quantity followed by *of*

It's important to know when to use *of* after expressions of quantity.

- use *of*:

a quarter *of*	*About a quarter of the class voted for football.*
ninety per cent *of*	*Over ninety per cent of us have brown eyes.*
two thirds *of*	*Two thirds of the class come to school by car.*

- *of* is optional:

  | half (of) | *Half (of) the class voted for English as their favourite subject.* |
  | all (of) | *All (of) the students in our group voted for blue as their favourite colour.* |

- *most* without *of*:

  | most | *Most students use the Internet.* |

- *most* with *of*:

  | most of | *Most of the students in our class use the Internet.* |
  | | *Most of us use the Internet.* |

Writing

2 Rewrite these survey findings using the expressions in the box.

| 40% | almost two thirds | half | all | a quarter | most |

1 17 out of 27 of the class go swimming once week.
Almost two thirds of the class go swimming once a week.
2 50% of us play the guitar.
3 25% of the students eat cereal for breakfast.
4 100% of the class voted for football as their favourite sport.
5 Eight out of twenty students chose oranges as their favourite fruit.
6 Seventeen out of twenty students get eight or more hours' sleep a night.

3 Use the expressions in Exercise 2 to talk about your own class survey.

Project: Design and carry out a survey

4 Design and illustrate your own survey using questions 11–20 in the class survey.

- Use your survey to interview the adults in your family.

Either

- Write a report of what the survey tells you.
  75% of the adults in the survey have coffee for breakfast.

or

- Use bar charts and pie charts to present the information.

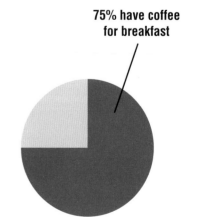
75% have coffee for breakfast

Fiction

1 Here are the key words from the story you're going to read. Match them with their meanings.

1 generous
2 to share
3 peasant
4 to steal
5 thief

6 drought
7 wealth
8 pleasure
9 poverty

a being poor
b to take what is not yours
c money and possessions
d to divide something between two or more people
e wanting to help people by giving them money
f enjoyment
g a person who steals
h a poor farmer
i a long period of time when there is no rain

2 Read about Vimal Shinagadia. Then read his story. Do you think it is based on real events and real people? Or is it a fable – a traditional story that teaches a moral lesson? Give your reasons.

> Vimal Shinagadia is 16 years old.
> 'My name is Vimal and I go to Whitefield School in London. This story is a traditional Hindi story and it was told to me by my friend's mother.'

3 Answer the questions.

1 How would you describe the character of the king in this story?
2 How would you describe the character of the peasant?
3 Could the story have ended differently?
4 Find five time expressions in the story. How do these time expressions help you when you're reading?
Once upon a time, …
5 How many times does the writer use the word 'gold'? Which other words does he use several times? Why do you think he repeats these words?
6 Fables and traditional tales often feature an action which is repeated. What is the action in this story which is repeated? What would have been different if this action had happened only once? Can you think of another traditional story where an action is repeated?

4 What is the moral of the story? Do you agree with it? Why?

To Give

Once upon a time, there was a very powerful and very generous king who gave much of his gold to the poor people of his lands. Each morning, the king would wake up early and share his gold with the poor people who had gathered at the gates of his palace so that they might buy food and clothing.

One night, a peasant crept up to the palace and huddled up against the wall where he would not be seen. The peasant decided that he would camp by the gates of the palace so that he would be the first in line to receive some gold pieces from the king the following morning. "If I am the first," reasoned the peasant, "then perhaps the king will give me more gold and I will no longer be poor or hungry."

But when one of the royal guards noticed the peasant creeping around at the gates of the palace, he thought that the man must be a thief come to steal the king's gold in the night. And so the guard captured the peasant and locked him away in the prison beneath the palace.

The next morning, after being told of the events of the previous night, the generous king decided to go and talk to the peasant who was locked in his prison.

The king approached the dark and damp cell and asked the peasant, "Why would you want to steal from me when all you had to do was ask for gold in order to feed and clothe yourself; do you not know that I would have given it to you gladly?"

The poor man explained that he was not a thief at all, but simply a peasant who had fallen on hard times and now needed help. "I was once a good farmer and a good businessman," said the man, "until the droughts came and thieves stole my cattle." The peasant looked directly at the king. "I did not come to steal from you," he insisted. "I came in the night so that I might be the first to receive some gold in the morning. That is all, I promise."

Upon hearing the peasant's story, the generous king was much moved. He ordered the guards to release the man from his prison. Then he gave the peasant ten gold pieces with which to change his fortunes. The peasant thanked the generous king and left the palace with his gold.

But the next day, the peasant was not satisfied with his gift of ten gold pieces. Each night he returned to the palace and waited by the gates, and each morning the generous king bestowed upon the peasant ten more gold pieces.

This went on for many nights and many days, until the king asked the peasant, "Why do you continue to come to my palace when I have given you so much gold? Surely you are no longer poor or hungry?"

"But I wish to be like you," said the peasant to the king. "I want to be rich and powerful."

"But will you also be generous to the poor of the land?" asked the king.

The peasant thought about this question for a few moments before he answered. 'Yes indeed I would, Your Majesty."

"Then I shall give you half of my kingdom and half of my riches," replied the king, "but you must promise me that you will always be generous to those who might need your help."

The peasant agreed, and so the king gave half of all his wealth and half of his entire kingdom.

The years passed quickly and the peasant proved to be a wise and generous man. He used much of his gold to plant food and raise cattle, and very soon he had doubled his riches and was able to share more and more wealth with the poor people of the land. The king watched from his palace and was very pleased with what he saw. He knew then that to give was the greatest pleasure there ever was in the world. By sharing what he owned with others, the generous king was able to make many people happy.

The peasant had learned this lesson well and he too shared his wealth and happiness with those around him. And very soon, because the king and the wise peasant both gave so generously, there was no more poverty or hunger in the whole of the land.

To Give, a Hindi Story by Vimal Shinagadia,
http://www.worldstories.org.uk/stories/story

Review of Units 9–10

Vocabulary

Sports

1 Use the verbs in the box to complete this report. Remember to use the correct tense.

> compete   take part   take place
> train   win

● SPORTS NEWS

The inter-schools athletics competition
___

We're pleased to report a good result in the inter-schools athletics competition. Our athletes *had trained*[1] very hard in the weeks leading up to the event, which _____[2] at the University athletics ground.

There were thirty students in our athletics team. The school band also _____[3] in the event, providing music throughout the afternoon. Our athletes _____[4] in all the events and _____[5] a total of fifteen medals, including first place in the 4 x 100 metres relay.

---

2 Read the descriptions of people involved in sports events. Who are they?

1 people who are good at sports   athletes
2 people who watch sports   s_____
3 people who take part in competitions   c_____
4 the best team or player   ch_____
5 the person you compete against   o_____
6 the person who takes first place in a competition   w_____

Maths

3 Match the symbols in the circle to the words in the square.

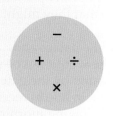

> add
> divide
> minus
> multiply
> plus
> subtract
> take away
> times

1 – minus, subtract, …

4 Label the shapes.

1 ☐ square   4

2 ○   5 ▭

3 △

Use of English

5 Write these sentences using the past simple and the past perfect.

1 He (*lose*) the match because he (*not practise*) enough.

   He lost the match because he hadn't practised enough.

2 I (*not play*) for a long time so I (*not win*) the tennis match.

3 She (*not be*) at home. She (*go*) to the gym.

4 We (*arrive*) late, but luckily the event (*not start*).

5 We (*not see*) the race because I (*left*) the tickets at home.

6 (*she / feel*) ill because (*she / not drink*) enough water?

6 Complete the sentences using a pronoun beginning with *every-*, *any-* or *no-*.

1 *Everyone* knows the answer to that question. It's really easy.
2 I've got tickets for Saturday's match. Is _____ interested?
3 I'm bored. There's _____ to do.
4 I didn't buy _____ because I hadn't got any money.
5 It was a really difficult maths problem. _____ got the answer right.
6 _____ can learn to ride a bike. It's simple!
7 He's really good at quizzes. He knows _____

7 Complete the sentences with a superlative adverb.

1 The winner of the javelin competition is the athlete who throws *the furthest*.
2 The 100 metres champion is the runner who runs _____ .
3 The high jump is won by the athlete who jumps _____ .
4 Until 2011, _____ anyone had ever run a marathon was 2 hours 3 minutes and 59 seconds.
5 Ellie Simmonds did well in the Paralympic 50 metres and 100 metres swimming, but she did _____ in the 200 metres.

8 Decide whether *the* is needed or not for each numbered space in the following text.

1 –, 2 the,

General knowledge quiz

9 Work with a partner. Answer the questions.

1 Why are the years 776 BCE and 1896 important in the history of the Olympic Games?
2 Wrestling was one of the sports in the ancient Olympic pentathlon. What were the other four?
3 What sort of race was a *stadion*?
4 Where did the ancient Olympic Games take place? Name the place and the country.
5 Who were not allowed to take part in the ancient Olympic Games?
6 When and where did the first Paralympics take place?
7 What is the popular name for this ratio: 1:1.618?
8 What is this building called and where is it?
9 Name one of the Seven Wonders of the Ancient World.
10 What are the Andes, the Pyrenees and the Himalayas?

A pocket guide to Spain

_____ [1] Spain is a country of contrasts. In _____ [2] north you can go skiing or mountain climbing in _____ [3] Pyrenees. You can enjoy the sunny beaches of _____ [4] Mediterranean, which are on _____ [5] east and south coast. Visit the Spanish islands – _____ [6] Balearics or _____ [7] Canaries – to find sun in winter. In Tenerife, you can climb _____ [8] Mount Teide. The capital, Madrid, is on _____ [9] central plateau. It's the highest capital city in _____ [10] Europe. Be sure to go to _____ [11] Prado to see paintings by Velázquez, Goya and Picasso. Don't miss _____ [12] Alhambra in Granada – the architecture is amazing and the gardens are wonderful.

11 We're going on holiday!

- **Topics** Types of holiday; holiday plans and experiences; airports; school exchanges
- **Use of English** Compound nouns; verbs followed by *-ing* form; reported speech – statements and questions

Holidays and places to stay

- What do you think of when you look at these photos?

Reading

1 Read the texts. How many of the following can you find?

- types of holiday accommodation
- holiday activities
- sports facilities
- features of the landscape

---

a I'm going to the coast with my family. We're staying at a hotel near a beach called Praia do Rosa. You can do lots of water sports like windsurfing and sailing there. You can go whale watching too. I'm really looking forward to it.

Bruno

b Most of the time I'm going to be at home, but I am going on a day trip with my family. We're going to Jeddah, which is right on the Red Sea coast. My cousins live there, so I can catch up with them. I'm looking forward to hearing all their news. We might go to the Al-Shallal theme park. You can go ice skating or roller skating there.

Mariam

c We're going camping. You can see Mount Fuji from the campsite. We went there last year and it was great. There are hot springs and tennis courts, and there's a big swimming pool. We're driving there, so we can take our tent with us. It isn't a long journey. It only takes two hours.

Ren

d I like going to other countries. You get a chance to see new things. We're flying to Dubrovnik and we're staying in an apartment. We're going on a half-day sightseeing tour when we get there. And there are islands to explore just off the coast, so we'll go on a boat trip to see them. I can't wait!

Anya

Use of English: Compound nouns

A compound noun is two nouns used together to describe one thing.

noun + noun

water sports = sports that you do on water

2 Use the words to make compound nouns.

boat	sightseeing	tour
courts	skating	trip
day	sports	watching
ice	swimming	water
park	tennis	whale
pool	theme	

Listening (21)

3 Listen to Joe, Amy, Sam and Tina talking about their holiday plans.

1 One student is staying at home. Where are the others going?
2 Where are they staying?
3 What are they planning to do?

Use of English: Verbs followed by *-ing* form

Use an *-ing* form after these verbs: *enjoy, don't mind*
I don't enjoy going on boat trips.

You can also use an *-ing* form after these verbs: *like, love, prefer*
I like staying at home.

---

4 Match the two halves of the sentences. Then write the numbers of the sentences that are true for you.

1 I like staying at home in the holidays because
2 I like going away during the holidays because
3 I don't enjoy going on boat trips because
4 I don't like going on long car journeys because
5 I love staying in a hotel
6 I don't mind sleeping in a tent.
7 I love going to theme parks because I enjoy the rides.
8 I don't really like going away on holiday.

a Camping is fun.
b I get bored at home.
c I get car sick.
d I can see all my friends.
e I get seasick.
f I prefer going on day trips.
g Some of them are quite scary!
h with a swimming pool.

Speaking

5 Use the sentences in Exercise 4 that were true for you to have a conversation with your partner about holidays.

A *I like going away during the holidays. I get bored at home.*
B *So do I. Where do you usually go?*
B *I don't enjoy going on boat trips.*
A *Nor do I. I get seasick.*
B *So do I. Do you get car sick too?*
A *No, I'm not too bad on long car journeys.*

Language tip

Agree with a positive statement
So do I. / So am I. / So would I.

Agree with a negative statement
Nor do I. / Nor am I. / Nor would I.

At the airport

- What signs do you expect to see at an international airport? Why do the signs have pictures on them?

 a

 b

 c

Vocabulary

1 Work with a partner. How quickly can you match the signs to their meanings?

1	check in	**7**	lift
2	departures	**8**	meeting point
3	arrivals	**9**	currency exchange
4	passport control	**10**	medical room
5	customs	**11**	Internet point
6	baggage reclaim	**12**	café

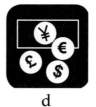 d

 e

 f

2 In pairs, take turns to give each other clues for the signs.

> A I've just arrived. Where do I go to collect my bags?

> B That's number 6: baggage reclaim

 g

 h

 i

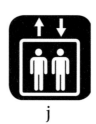 j

 k

 l

Reading

3 Read the text messages. Who is travelling? Where is she? Who's meeting her?

1
Hi Daniel
I'm at the airport.
I had a terrible journey. I missed the bus! I'm waiting in the check-in queue.
Anya

2
Hi Halina
I'm sitting in the departures lounge, so I can relax for a few minutes.
Anya

3
Hi Lara
I want to buy you a present, but I haven't got much time.
Anya

4
Hi Luka
The gate number is already up on the screen, so I don't think the plane will be late.
I'll text you when I arrive.
Anya

5
Hi Sacha
I'm just getting on the plane. I'll see you in Arrivals.
Anya

6
Hi Sacha
Have you heard from Anya yet?
Mum

7
Hi Mum
Yes, she said she was just getting on the plane and she would see us in Arrivals.
Sacha

Use of English: Reported speech – statements

When we tell people what someone said, we usually change the tense, because what they said was in the past.

direct speech	tense change	reported speech
Anya:		Anya's friends:
'I'm at the airport.'	am / are / is → was / were	She said she was at the airport.
'I'm sitting in the departures lounge.'		She said she was sitting in the departures lounge.
'I haven't got much time.'	have / has → had	She said she hadn't got much time.
'I can relax.'	can → could	She said she could relax.
'I'll see you in Arrivals.'	will → would	She said she would see us in Arrivals.
'I don't think the plane will be late.'	do / does → did	She said she didn't think the plane would be late.
'I want to buy you a present.'	present simple → past simple	She said she wanted to buy me a present.
'I had a terrible journey.'	past simple → past perfect	She said she had had a terrible journey.

4 Study the chart for one minute. Then work with a partner. Cover the last column of the chart (reported speech). Take it in turns to report Anya's words.

5 Report the other things that Anya said. Use the chart above to help you.

1 'I missed the bus.'   *She said she'd missed the bus.*
2 'I'm waiting in the check-in queue.'   *She said …*
3 'The gate number is already up on the screen.'   *She said …*
4 'I'll text you when I arrive.'   *She said …*
5 'I'm just getting on the plane.'   *She said …*

Writing

6 Imagine you are at an airport. Write five texts to your friends, beginning:

1 I'm …   2 I had …   3 I saw …   4 There's …   5 I'll …

Speaking

7 Pass your texts to another member of your group. He/She has to report what you said.

He / She said he / she was …

A school exchange trip

● Are school exchange trips a good idea?

Reading

1 Look at the photo and read Carter's blog. Match each of the students' questions to a sentence in the blog.

I went on a school exchange trip to Mexico last month. I took a photo of my class. The students asked me how old I was. They asked me where I was staying, how long I would stay in Mexico, why I had decided to come to Mexico and what I watched on TV.
They asked me if I was American (!), if I liked football and if I could play an instrument.
They asked me a lot of questions!

Carter   Toronto, Canada

Use of English: Reported speech – questions

When we tell people what someone asked, we usually change the tense, because what they said was in the past. We also need to change the word order.

Questions that begin with a question word *(What, Where, When, Who, Why, How etc.)*

How old are you? → *They asked me how old I was.*

    NOT   ~~They asked me how old was I.~~

Why did you decide to come to Mexico? → *They asked me why I had decided to come to Mexico.*

    NOT   ~~They asked me why had I decided to come to Mexico.~~

Notice that we don't use *do* in reported questions:

What do you watch on TV? → *They asked me what I watched on TV.*

Yes / No questions

To report *Yes / No* questions, use *if*:

Are you American? → *They asked me if I was American.*
Do you like football? → *They asked me if I liked football.*

2 Here are some more of the students' questions. What did they ask Carter?

What's your name?   *They asked him …*
Where do you live?
What kind of food do you like?

3 Report these questions. Remember to use *if*.

Are you good at football?   *They asked him …*
Do you like Mexican food?
Can you speak French?

Writing and speaking

4 Write six questions for your partner. Use these ideas.

1 Where have you been on holiday …?	● recently ● in the last year
2 Where are you going …?	● next summer ● for your next holiday ● this weekend
3 What do you …?	● do on holiday? ● miss ● enjoy doing ● hate doing
4 Have you been …?	● to Brazil ● to a safari park ● on a sailing holiday
5 Can you …?	● surf ● scuba dive ● windsurf
6 Have you ever stayed …?	● at a campsite ● in a big hotel ● on a small island

Work in pairs. Ask and answer the questions. Then report your conversation to the class.

Writing

5 Rewrite the postcard below, putting in the correct punctuation.

Language tip

- Use a capital letter at the beginning of a sentence, for *I*, and for names of people and places.
- Add apostrophes for missing letters (*he's, I've*) and for the possessive *s* (*my mum's sister*).

im having a great time here im staying at a camping resort in the forest with my friends family we went on a boat trip on the river li yesterday today theres a day trip to the hot springs at longsheng see you soon love yuan

Project: A special treat

6 Plan a special holiday treat for a friend or for a member of your family.

- Write your plan:

  I'd like to take my mum / dad / best friend to … We'll go in … (January / April / the summer) We'll go for … (a day trip / a weekend / a fortnight) We'll fly to … We'll travel by … (car / train)

- Present your plan to the class. Use pictures to illustrate your plan if possible.

- Answer questions from other students about your holiday treat.

- **Topics** The weather; global warming and extreme weather; a zero-carbon city
- **Use of English** Present simple active and passive in scientific writing

The weather

- Think of symbols you've seen on a weather map or weather forecast. Describe them.

Vocabulary

1 Match the weather forecast extracts to these symbols.

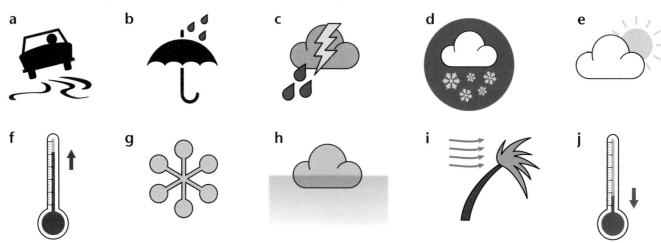

1 It'll be wet tomorrow. There'll be thunderstorms and heavy rain.
2 It will be windy all day but with strong winds in the late afternoon.
3 Tomorrow morning we'll see a heavy frost in most areas.
4 Temperatures will fall rapidly this evening.
5 Temperatures will rise to 40°C during the course of the day.
6 It will be cloudy with sunny intervals.

7 There will be icy conditions on the roads in the morning.
8 There may be one or two light showers towards the end of the afternoon.
9 Early-morning mist in coastal areas will clear slowly.
10 With clear skies and a good chance of snow tomorrow over high ground, it's good news for skiers.

2 Make collocations by finding the adjectives which go with these nouns. They are all in Exercise 1.

1	*heavy*	rain, frost	6	_____	areas
2	_____	winds	7	_____	skies
3	_____	intervals	8	a _____	chance
4	_____	conditions	9	_____	ground
5	_____	showers	10	_____	news

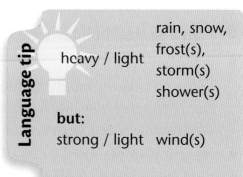

Language tip

heavy / light — rain, snow, frost(s), storm(s), shower(s)

but:
strong / light — wind(s)

Listening (22)

3 What would you expect to hear in a weather forecast for tomorrow in your country?

4 Listen to the weather forecast for Spain. Does the map show the weather for the early morning or the afternoon?

5 Listen again and complete the notes.

	6 am	**3 pm**
central and west	*low*[1] temperatures early-morning _____[2]	mostly _____[3] occasional cloud temperature: 10 degrees
north-west	wet and _____[4]	wet and windy _____[5] intervals temperature _____[6] degrees
north	heavy_____[7], _____[8] and icy conditions over higher ground temperature: minus 5 degrees to 6 degrees	
east	sunny	_____[9] with sunny intervals temperature: 12 to _____[10] degrees
south	_____[11] skies, lots of sunshine, a _____[12] wind in coastal areas temperature: 19 degrees	

Speaking

6 Work with a partner. Use your notes from Exercise 5 and take it in turns to give the weather forecast for Spain. Try to use the collocations you found in Exercise 2.

Tomorrow, in the north-west, it will be wet and windy, but in the afternoon there will be sunny intervals …

Writing

7 Choose an area of your country and write the weather forecast for that area.

In the east the day will start well with …

Language tip

It will be … rainy, windy, wet, cloudy, sunny, frosty, snowy.

There will be … rain, wind, cloud, clear skies, sunshine, frost, snow.

Extreme weather

- What is 'extreme weather'? Can you think of some examples?

Reading

1 Read the article. Think of a title. What does the diagram show?

Heatwaves, floods, hurricanes, tornadoes and droughts are nothing new, but there have been a lot of them in recent years. Why?

In the last 50 years, the average global temperature has risen by 0.5°C. Most scientists believe that this global warming is one of the main reasons for the increase in extreme weather.

As the earth's oceans become warmer, more moisture evaporates into the air. The extra moisture in the air causes heavier rain, more storms and floods.

The rise in temperature makes dry areas, with low rainfall, even drier and can turn them into deserts.

So what causes global warming? The sun warms the earth. Its rays pass through the earth's atmosphere and they are reflected back out to space. The atmosphere is made of gases. Some of these are called 'greenhouse gases'. The gases form a protective layer which helps to control the heat passing to and from the earth, and keeps it at the right temperature for animals, plants and humans.

Today we use a lot of fuel to heat our houses, to drive our cars and to run our factories. This produces carbon dioxide (CO_2) which adds to the layer of gases in the atmosphere. The layer is getting thicker and too much heat is kept in the earth's atmosphere. So the earth gets hotter and that's when global warming becomes a problem.

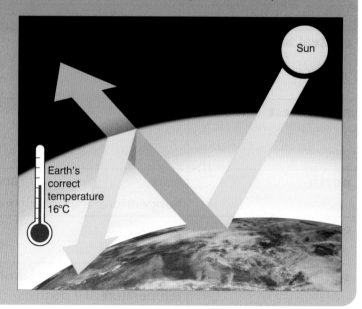

Sun

Earth's correct temperature 16°C

Vocabulary

2 Match these words from the text to their definitions.

1	heatwave	a	a large amount of water that covers an area which is normally dry
2	flood	b	a long period of time when there is no rain
3	hurricane	c	a very strong and dangerous wind that blows in a circle
4	tornado	d	a violent storm with very strong winds
5	drought	e	higher than normal temperatures lasting for several days
6	moisture	f	the gases around the earth
7	to evaporate	g	thin straight lines of light (from the sun)
8	rays	h	to change from a liquid into a gas
9	the atmosphere	i	very small drops of water in the air
10	reflected	j	when light or heat is sent back out into space

3 Work with a partner. Answer the questions.

1 Why is there more interest today in extreme weather?
2 What has happened to the temperature of the earth?
3 What's the connection between the oceans getting warmer and heavier rainfall?
4 What effect does global warming have on dry areas?
5 Why is the layer of gases round the earth necessary?
6 What causes too much global warming?

Use of English: Present simple active and passive (in scientific writing)

In scientific and technical writing, the passive is often used. This is because we focus on the action, not the person or the thing that does the action.

Present simple active
As the earth's oceans become warmer, more moisture evaporates into the air.

Present simple passive
The atmosphere is made of gases. Some of these are called greenhouse gases.

**Find two more examples of the present simple passive in the text in Exercise 1.
Is it possible to make them active?**

4 Complete the sentences using the present simple.
Put one verb in the active and one in the passive.

1 Sounds *are made* when objects *vibrate*. (*make, vibrate*)
2 When water _____ to 100°C, it _____ . (*heat, boil*)
3 When water _____ , it _____ . (*heat, evaporate*)
4 Water _____ ice when it _____ to 0°C. (*become, cool*)
5 A liquid _____ into a gas when it _____ . (*evaporate, heat*)
6 When metals _____ they _____ . (*heat, expand*)

Listening (23)

5 What do you know about thunder and lightning? Share your ideas with other students.

6 Work with a partner. Write your answers to these questions then listen and check.

1 In a thunderstorm, is lightning always followed by thunder?
2 How is the noise of thunder produced?
3 Do thunderstorms happen more often in hot climates than in cold climates?
4 The sound of thunder is measured in decibels. On average, it's about 120 decibels. What is the temperature of lightning measured in? How hot is it?
5 How do you tell how far away a thunderstorm is?

7 In groups, ask and answer the questions in Exercise 6. Make your answers as detailed as possible.

The world's first zero-carbon city

● What do you think a 'zero-carbon' city is?

Reading

1 Read the article about Masdar. Why is the city good news for the environment?

> Masdar is the world's first zero-carbon city. It is in Abu Dhabi and it is designed to be free of cars and skyscrapers. It is powered by the sun and cooled by the wind.

The city, which is only a few years old, combines traditional architecture with twenty-first century engineering: the best of the past is combined with the best of the future.

In some ways, Masdar is like an ancient Arabic city: it is surrounded by a wall and the streets are narrow so that the houses, which are not more than four or five storeys high, shade each other. The temperature in the street is 12° to 15°C cooler than in other cities.

The desert's natural resources – sun and wind – are used instead of the more traditional resources such as oil. There are wind towers which draw the wind down into the streets to help cool the air. Solar panels provide solar energy.

There are no cars in the city, but you can travel on the personal rapid transit system. You get into a pod, press the button and off you go. There is no driver. The network is powered by solar energy, so it produces no carbon dioxide (CO_2). The pods are programmed to go where you ask. They can travel at up to 40 kilometres an hour. Masdar will be home to about 50,000 people, at least 1000 businesses, two hotels and a university.

An international team of architects and engineers are working with the forces of nature to provide a model for the city of the future.

Vocabulary

2 What are these scientific and technical words in your language?

1 zero-carbon
2 engineering
3 natural resources
4 temperature
5 solar panels
6 solar energy
7 network
8 carbon dioxide

3 Find the words in the text for the following:

1 very tall buildings   *skyscrapers*
2 following the way things have been done for a long time
3 very old
4 the floors of a house
5 to protect from the sun
6 in place of
7 companies, places of work

4 Decide whether these statements about Masdar are true or false.

1 There were zero-carbon cities before Masdar.   *False*
2 There are no tall houses.
3 It's a very old city.
4 Oil is needed to produce energy there.
5 It's powered by renewable energy.
6 You can drive in the city.
7 You will be able to live and work there.
8 You'll be able to study there.

5 Read the comments about Masdar. Which are positive and which are negative?

1 Brilliant! You can live, work and go to school all in the same place.
2 Let's improve the cities we've got instead of spending so much money on new ones.
3 I can't imagine living in a city without a car.
4 I hope the architects and engineers are going to build cities like Masdar in other places.
5 In the twenty-first century, using renewable energy resources has to be the answer.
6 I'm not sure about the idea of living so close to other people. I think people need space.

Speaking

6 Work in small groups. Which of the comments in Exercise 5 do you agree with? Why?

Project: An eco house

7 What are eco houses? Find out, and give a presentation of one.

Stage 1

Make notes on:
- where it is
- what eco features it has (solar panels, etc.)
- what other special features it has
- what you like about it.

Stage 2

Find some pictures to illustrate your project.

Stage 3

Give an illustrated talk to the class about your eco house.

Poetry

1 If you were going to write a poem about the weather, what kind of weather would you choose and why?

2 Read *Rain Falls Down*. The stressed syllables in the first two verses have been marked to help you read the poem with the correct rhythm.

Rain Falls Down

The clouds begin to rub together
soft as the stroke of a silky feather
then the rain begins to fall

the rain falls down
like tip tip tapping
the rain falls down
like clap clap clapping
and the rain comes falling down

the rain falls down
tumbling under
the rain falls down
like the sound of thunder
and the rain comes falling down

the rain comes down
like the sound of thunder
the rain falls down
tumbling under
and the rain comes falling down

the rain falls down
like the sound of clapping

the rain falls down
like tip tip tapping

the clouds begin to rub together
soft as the stroke of a silky feather
and the SUN comes out again

Margot Henderson

The <u>clouds</u> be<u>gin</u> to <u>rub</u> to<u>gether</u>
<u>soft</u> <u>as</u> the <u>stroke</u> of a <u>silky</u> <u>feather</u>
<u>then</u> the <u>rain</u> be<u>gins</u> to <u>fall</u>

the <u>rain</u> falls <u>down</u>
like <u>tip</u> tip <u>tapping</u>
the <u>rain</u> falls <u>down</u>
like <u>clap</u> clap <u>clapping</u>
and the <u>rain</u> comes <u>falling</u> <u>down</u>

rub to press or move one object against another

stroke a gentle movement, often of your hand, across the surface of something

tapping knocking lightly on, for example, a window or a door; in the poem, *tip tip tapping* describes the sound of light rain

clapping the sound you make when you hit your hands together; in the poem *clap clap clapping* describes the sound of heavy rain

tumbling falling quickly and suddenly with a rolling movement

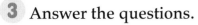

3 Answer the questions.

1 What do you notice about the rhythm of the poem? Does it change from verse to verse? Is it a strong rhythm?
2 Is repetition a feature of this poem? Give examples.
3 Why are rhythm and repetition important in this poem?
4 If you could draw a line to represent this poem, what would it look like?

5 If you were including this poem in a book, what kind of picture would you choose to illustrate it?

4 Read *Your Dresses*. Is it about a person and what they're wearing? Is it about someone's personality, or their moods? Is it about different kinds of weather? Or is it about all of these?

Your Dresses

I like your rain dress,
its strange, sad colour,
its small buttons like tears.

I like your fog dress,
how it swirls around you
when you dance on the lawn.

Your snow dress I like,
its million snowflakes
sewn together with a needle of ice.

But I like your thunderstorm dress,
its huge, dark petticoats,
its silver stitches flashing as you run away.

Carol Ann Duffy

5 Answer these questions.

1 How does the poet represent:
  a raindrops?
  b thunderclouds?
  c lightning?
2 Which is more important in this poem, the sound of the words or the images (pictures) they create? Is the same true of the first poem, *Rain Falls Down*?
3 What images do you see when you read *Your Dresses*? Exchange ideas with your partner.

tears drops of water that come from your eyes when you cry
swirl move around quickly in circles
lawn an area of ground in a garden which is covered with short grass
snowflakes small pieces of falling snow
sewn (past participle of sew) joined with a needle and thread
needle a small thin piece of metal with a point at one end and a hole at the other, used for sewing
petticoats long skirts that were worn under a skirt or dress by women in the past
stitches the small pieces of thread that you can see on cloth that has been sewn

Review of Units 11–12
Vocabulary
Holidays

1 Match a word from column A with a word from column B to make compound nouns.

A	B
sightseeing	sports
tennis	skating
day	court
ice	trip
swimming	tour
theme	pool
water	park

sightseeing tour

2 Label these airport signs using the words in the box.

café	check in
passport control	arrivals
customs	lift
departures	currency exchange
meeting point	baggage reclaim

3 Where do you go?

1 You want to get your boarding pass and hand over your luggage. *You go to check in.*

2 You want to go up to the fifth floor and you have a lot of luggage.

3 Your friends' flight has just arrived. You've arranged to meet them.

4 You want to change some money.

5 You want to collect your luggage.

Weather

4 Match the weather symbols to the descriptions.

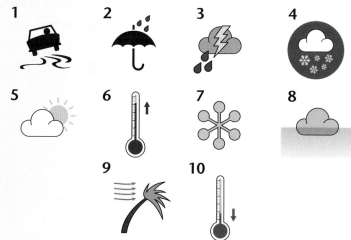

a cloudy with sunny intervals
b frost
c ice
d temperature falling
e temperature rising
f mist
g showers
h snow
i strong winds
j thunder and heavy rain

Use of English

5 **Complete the sentences using the verbs in the box in the *-ing* form.**

fly	go	sail	sleep	spend
stay	swim	try	visit	

1 My mum doesn't like *flying*.
2 I don't mind _____ in a tent, but I prefer _____ in an apartment.
3 Do you enjoy _____ the whole day on the beach?
4 I love _____ in the sea. It's much more fun than in a pool.
5 I like _____ new food when I'm on holiday.
6 I enjoy _____ new places on holiday.
7 Do your parents like _____ on activity holidays?
8 My dad doesn't enjoy _____ because he gets seasick.

6 **Report these questions.**

1 'Are you here on holiday?'
   She asked me if I was here on holiday.
2 'Where are you staying?'
   She asked me where I was staying.
3 'Are you having a good time?'
4 'Is the surfing good?'
5 'Have you been on a boat trip?'
6 'Which beach do you like best?'
7 'Have you tried the beach café?'
8 'Do you want to play beach volleyball this afternoon?'

7 **Report what Ben said about his holiday.**

1 'I had a great time.'
   He said he'd had a great time.
2 'I met somebody from school there.'
   He said …
3 'I've learned to surf.'
   He said …
4 'I want to learn to windsurf now.'
   He said …
5 'I stayed at a great campsite near the beach.'
   He said …
6 'I'll definitely go back, but I don't know when.'
   He said …
7 'I'm having a party on Saturday.'
   He said …
8 'We can catch up then.'
   He said …

8 **Complete the sentences by using a verb from the box in the present passive. Use *by* when necessary.**

call	follow	heat	make	measure

1 Thunder is the sound that *is made by* lightning.
2 Lightning _____ thunder.
3 When lightning passes through the atmosphere, the air _____ very quickly and expands.
4 The sound of the air expanding _____ thunder.
5 The temperature of lightning _____ in degrees Celsius.

13 In and out of school

- **Topics** Education and learning styles; international penpals
- **Use of English** Prepositions followed by the *-ing* form (*get into trouble for talking*); verbs followed by the infinitive with *to*

What helps you to learn?

- Do you like working in groups or do you prefer working on your own? Are there times when it's good to talk in a lesson?

Reading

1 Read the comments on this website about talking in class. Who thinks it's a good idea, and why?

> ### " Talking in class
>
> **You might get into trouble for chatting in class, but education experts have found that talking to your classmates can be helpful. 'Students should be encouraged to explain things to each other and to discuss things,' they say.**
>
> Sometimes you're scared of asking the teacher, so I often ask a classmate instead of interrupting the teacher.
>
> **Naimul**
>
> Talking in class distracts you from getting on with your work. I get tired of telling people to be quiet.
>
> **Sumaya**
>
> At the end of the lesson, our teacher lets us talk about what we've learned in class. I think that's a good idea. It helps us to remember what we've done and we can ask questions.
>
> **Iñigo**
>
> Our teacher sometimes tells us off for talking in class. It's true that if you're talking too much, you won't hear what the teacher is saying, so you won't learn anything.
>
> **Rahma**
>
> Sharing ideas with friends helps me to learn. And you can learn by comparing answers.
>
> **Tammy**
>
> We are not allowed to talk during important subjects like Science and Maths, but we can in subjects like Art and DT. That seems OK to me. You can paint and talk, but you can't do experiments with dangerous acids and talk at the same time. You need to concentrate on doing the experiments carefully!
>
> **Iqra**
>
> I often get into trouble for talking too much. That's why I like my Spanish lessons. You have to talk a lot because you need to practise speaking Spanish.
>
> **Chloe** "

Speaking

2 Read the comments in Exercise 1 again. Who do you agree with? Who do you disagree with?

I agree with Tammy. Sharing ideas with friends helps me to learn.

Writing

3 Complete the sentences with the correct preposition and the *-ing* form of the verb.

of (× 2)	for (× 2)	from	on
instead of	by		

1 You learn _____ (*do*).   *You learn by doing.*
2 I get tired _____ (*learn*) dates in History.
3 I sometimes take the bus to school _____ (*walk*).
4 I'm not scared _____ (*ask*) questions in class.
5 Listening to music doesn't distract me _____ (*do*) my homework.
6 I can't concentrate _____ (*do*) my work when there's a lot of noise in the class.
7 Our teacher sometimes tells us off _____ (*be*) too noisy.
8 I often get into trouble _____ (*forget*) my book.

4 Choose some sentences from Exercise 3 and change them, so that they are true for you.

Use of English: Prepositions followed by *-ing*

We use *-ing* forms after prepositions:

preposition   *-ing* form

I sometimes get into trouble for talking in class.

Speaking

5 What helps you to learn? How do you learn best? Discuss in groups.

1 What helps you to concentrate when you're doing your homework?
A *Listening to music helps me to concentrate. What about you?*
B *No, I can't concentrate with music playing; I like having a quiet place to work.*
2 What helps you when you're in class?
3 What sort of learner are you? Can you remember things without writing them down?
4 In practical subjects, do you learn by doing or can you understand how to do something by reading about it?

Writing

6 Write a short paragraph about how you learn best. Use the questions in Exercise 5 to help you.

I always listen to music when I'm doing my homework. It helps me to concentrate …

Freedom to learn

- Look at the picture below. What does it show?

Reading and listening 24

1 Read about Summerhill School. What kind of school is it?

SUMMERHILL SCHOOL in Suffolk, England, opened in 1921. It was very different from other schools because children had much more freedom there. Since that time, schools around the world have followed the Summerhill 'free school' model.

LEARNING AT A 'FREE SCHOOL'
Summerhill is for 5- to 18-year-olds. There is a timetable which includes all the usual academic subjects, but all lessons are optional: students only go to lessons that interest them. If they prefer to do something different, they can go to the art room, the woodwork room or the computer room; they learn to make their own decisions. If students want to take exams, they can. However, exams are not compulsory.

2 True or false?
1 Summerhill School is almost a hundred years old.   *True*
2 There are schools like Summerhill in other countries.
3 Summerhill is for young as well as older children.
4 Students have to go to all the lessons on the timetable.
5 Students don't have to take exams.

3 Listen and find out more about Summerhill. Which two aspects of the school does the speaker talk about?

4 Listen again. True or false?
1 It's difficult to find somewhere to play in your free time.
2 There are lots of outdoor activities you can do at the school.
3 There are school meetings once a week.
4 You can only discuss school rules at the school meeting.
5 The meeting has a different chairman each week.
6 The students can change the school rules.

La Cecilia, Argentina

Use of English: Verbs followed by the infinitive with *to*

1 verb + *to* infinitive

After some verbs we use an infinitive with *to*:
agree, begin, continue, decide, forget, hope, learn, remember, start, try
They learn to make their own decisions.

2 verb (+ object) + *to* infinitive

After the following verbs you can put an object between the verb and the *to* infinitive:
ask, choose, expect, help, like, prefer, promise, want
They expect to come to the meeting.
They expect you to come to the meeting.

After the following verbs you must use an object between the verb and the
to infinitive: allow, encourage, invite, teach, tell

Language tip

After *begin, continue, start* and *prefer*, you can also use the *-ing* form of the verb.

Writing

5 Complete the sentences using the verbs in brackets. Remember to use the infinitive with *to*.

1 **A** Can you windsurf?
   B Yes, I had lessons at the school summer camp.
   I learned to windsurf at the school summer camp.   (learn)

2 **A** Shall we play football or shall we start on our project?
   B Let's play football.
   We had some school work to do, but we _____   (decide)

3 If I have the chance, I'll go to university to study Medicine.
   I _____   (hope)

4 We said we'd meet at 4 o'clock.
   We _____   (agree)

5 I'm sure your teacher will explain the homework. Ask her.
   Ask your teacher to explain the homework.   (ask)

6 I'd really like to be able to make a tortilla. Can you show me?
   Can you _____   (teach)

7 Our English teacher says we'll do well in our exam.
   Our English teacher _____   (expect)

8 The sports teacher said I should join a team.
   The sports teacher _____   (encourage)

Speaking

6 Answer these questions.

1 What are the main differences between your school and a school like Summerhill?

2 Are 'free schools' a good idea? Discuss these statements.

● You can choose to go to class or to do something else.
   A *I think that's a good idea because you only go the lessons that interest you.*
   B *I think it's a bad idea because some people are lazy. They won't go to any lessons. They'll just play all the time.*

● Students are expected to take responsibility for their own learning.

● Some students prefer to concentrate on creative and practical subjects like art and woodwork, and they're free to do that.

Friends across the world

- What's good about having friends in other countries?

Reading

1 Read Tina's letter on page 109. Why is she writing to someone at Hill Top School?

Speaking

2 Work with a partner. What do you have in common with Tina?

3 Read this letter from Matt. What do you have in common with Matt? Matt mentions white-water rafting. Tell your partner about something you've done recently.

Dear Friend

My name is Matt and I'm 12 years old. I live in Richmond, near London, and I go to Hill Top School. My favourite subjects are English, Science, Maths and cooking. I really love my school. I like going to the after-school clubs; my favourite is indoor rowing. I'm also in the choir.

I recently went on a white-water rafting weekend with the Boat Club that I go to on a Thursday evening. We went to Devon, but, unfortunately, I hurt my knee and had to have an operation. I have to be in a wheelchair for the next six weeks.

I would love to find out all about you, so please write back to me.

Matt

Project: Letter to a penpal

4 You're going to write a letter to a new penpal. Introduce yourself and give information about your life. Use either Tina's letter or Matt's letter as a model.

Tina Yu is a student at Minsheng Junior High School in Taipei, Taiwan. Her school has a link with a secondary school in east London.

Dear friend from Hill Top School,

Hello! My name is Tina Yu. Nice to meet you. I'm a seventh grader from Minsheng Junior High School.

Here are my answers to your questions:

1. **Q: What type of food do you like?**

   A: We eat all kinds of food, like rice, noodles, bread, milk, fruit, vegetables, pizza.

2. **Q: How do you travel around your city?**

   A: Some of us take buses, taxis, the MRT [Metropolitan Rapid Transit] to travel around our city. Some of us travel around the city in our parents' car.

3. **Q: What lessons do you do in school?**

   A: We have Chinese, English, PE, Maths, Music, Health Education, Art, Biology, Geography, History, Performing Arts, Civic Education, Scout Education, Home Economics, counselling and career planning. We also have community activities and club activities.

4. **Q: Do you like English football?**

   A: I know what English football is, but I have never watched a whole game, and I don't know a lot about the rules.

5. **Q: What do you do in your spare time?**

   A: I read novels, watch movies or go out.

6. **Q: Do you have a lot of technology in your schools?**

   A: Yes, we have a computer room and there are TVs and projectors in the classrooms.

7. **Q: What's your house like?**

   A: My family live in an apartment. There is a living room, three bedrooms, a dining room, a kitchen, two bathrooms and a balcony. My grandma grows some plants on the balcony.

8. **Q: What are your cities like?**

   A: I live in Taipei. Living in my community is very convenient. There are a lot of trees and parks in Minsheng Community. We also have a lot of restaurants and shops.

9. **Q: Do you play any sports?**

   A: Yes, I swim, run, play tennis, play basketball and baseball and I go roller skating.

I hope to get your letter soon!!

Goodbye

Tina Yu

- **Topics** Shops and services; town and country; you and your community
- **Use of English** *to have something done*; *if* clauses to describe imaginary situations

Places in town

- Which is your favourite shop? Why?

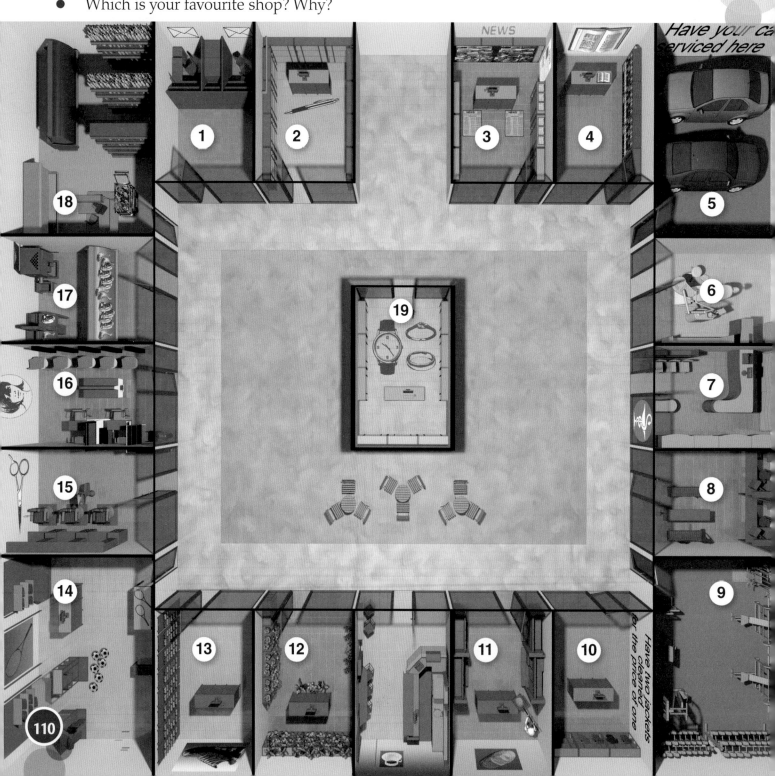

Vocabulary

1 Match the shops and services to the places on the plan.

11 e (bakery)

a	barber's	**f**	florist's	**k**	newsagent's	**p**	gym
b	dry cleaner's	**g**	jeweller's	**l**	stationery shop	**q**	post office
c	chemist's / pharmacy	**h**	butcher's	**m**	bookshop	**r**	bank
d	hairdresser's	**i**	shoe shop	**n**	sports shop	**s**	garage
e	bakery	**j**	supermarket	**o**	dentist's		

Speaking and vocabulary

2 Work with a partner. Say which shops and services there are near your school. Add information if you can.

A *There's a bakery in the High Street.*
B *Where?*
A *Next to the café. They sell nice cakes there.*
B *Is there a barber's near here?*

A *Yes, there's one opposite the bank. I have my hair cut there. Is there a dry cleaner's?*
B *I don't know. Is there a …*

3 Complete the sentences with the correct shop or service.

You can have your …

1 shopping delivered by the *supermarket*.
2 clothes cleaned at the _____.
3 hair cut at the _____ or _____.
4 feet measured at the _____.

5 car repaired at the _____.
6 teeth checked at the _____.
7 tennis racket repaired at the _____.
8 parcels weighed at the _____.

Use of English: *to have something done*

If you have something done, someone does it for you. You don't do it yourself.

`have` + `object` + `past participle`

I have my hair cut at the barber's opposite the bank.

---

4 Complete the paragraph about Stella Stardust, using the past participles of the verbs in the box.

clean	deliver	design	wash	make	prepare	repair

I have my clothes *designed*[1] in Paris. I have my shoes _____[2] in Italy. I have my hair _____[3] every day. I have fresh flowers _____[4] to my hotel room, wherever I am. I have all my meals _____[5] by my own chefs. I have my car _____[6] every day. I never have anything _____[7]; I just throw things away when they go wrong, or when I'm tired of them. Am I happy? No, I'm not. I'm bored. I never do anything for myself.

Town or country?

- Which words and phrases do you think of when you look at the photos on this page?

Reading

1 Read the opinions. Who do you agree with?

DO YOU PREFER THE COUNTRY OR THE CITY?

I live in the country and I love the freedom you have there. You can go on bike rides. You can swim in the lake in summer. You can have picnics. I feel a bit frightened when I'm in the city. It's so crowded – all those people everywhere!

Tasha

In the city, you can walk everywhere, or you can get a bus, and all the shops and things you need are there. But I like the country for holidays because it's nice and quiet.

Adil

If I had the choice, I would prefer to live in the city because there are lots of shops, places to eat and loads of other things. In the country there's nothing to do for people my age. It's quite boring!!

Joss

I used to live in a small village and I liked it a lot better there! Now, we live in a big city. It's so busy – more traffic, more pollution and more noise! There's more crime too. If I lived in the country, I'd ride my bike to school, but it's too dangerous in the city.

Kaher

I live in the country and I love it. There are lots of nice walks to go on and it's quiet. The city is too noisy, busy and smoky for me! When I go to sleepovers in the city, I can't get to sleep for the noise.

Tara

Would I like to live in the country if I had the chance? I would and I wouldn't. I would because it's very quiet; I wouldn't because there's nothing to do. I'd like to live in the country, but near a big city. That way, I'd have the best of both worlds.

Nisha

I live a long way from any city and 17 miles from the nearest town. It takes half an hour to get to the nearest shop or to see my friends. You can't go to the cinema because it's too far away. You have to get your parents to take you places in the car. I wouldn't want to live in the city, though. It makes me tired when I go there and it's noisy and dirty.

Robert

2 Read the opinions again and answer the questions.

1 Who prefers the city?
2 Who prefers the country?
3 Who can see the advantages of both?

3 Look at these sentences from the text. Find another way of saying them by replacing the underlined words.

1 You have <u>to get</u> your parents to take you places in the car.
You have *to ask / persuade* your parents to take you places in the car.

2 I <u>used to live</u> in a small village.

3 <u>I liked it a lot better</u> there.

4 I can't get to sleep <u>for</u> the noise.

5 I'd have <u>the best of both worlds</u>.

6 <u>It takes</u> half an hour to get to the nearest shop.

Vocabulary

4 Use these adjectives and nouns to describe the place where you live.

- friendly / unfriendly
- clean / dirty / smoky
- quiet / noisy / busy / crowded
- boring / interesting / exciting

- traffic
- pollution
- noise
- crime

There's quite a lot of traffic during the day, but it's nice and quiet at night.

5 Use *if* + past tense and *would* to write these sentences.

1 If I (*have*) enough money, I (*buy*) a house by the beach for my family.

If I had enough money, I'd buy a house by the beach for my family.

2 I (*ride*) my bike every day if I (*live*) in the country.

3 If you (*have*) the choice, where (*you / like*) to live?

4 If we (*move*) to a big city, we (*not know*) anyone.

5 (*you / cycle*) to school if there (*be*) less traffic?

> **Use of English: The second conditional**
>
> We can use *if* clauses to describe imaginary situations.
>
>
> | Clause 1 | | Clause 2 |
> | *If* + past tense | | *would* |
>
> *If I lived in the country, I'd ride my bike to school.*
>
> You can change the order of the clauses like this:
>
> *I'd ride my bike to school if I lived in the country.*
> Remember that *I'd* is the short form of *I would*.
>
> You make questions and short answers like this:
>
> *Would I like to live in the country if I had the chance?*
> *I would and I wouldn't.*

Speaking and writing

6 Work in groups. Where would you like to live when you're an adult? Give your reasons. Then write a paragraph giving your opinion.

If I had the choice, I'd prefer to live in the city because there's more to do there.

If I had the choice, I would prefer to live … , because …
If I lived in the country / city, I'd …
I wouldn't want to live in …, because …

You and your community

- What do people in your community do to help each other?

Reading

1 Read the test 'How responsible are you?'. Choose a, b or c.

How responsible are you?

1 If I was sitting on a bus and I saw several old people standing, …
  a I'd stand up and give one of them my seat.
  b I'd wait until I got near my stop and then I'd give them my seat.
  c I wouldn't do anything, because perhaps they're not very old.

2 If I saw someone dropping litter in the street, …
  a I'd pick it up and put it in a bin.
  b I'd say: 'Excuse me, I think you've dropped something.'
  c I'd tell a policeman.

3 If your friend was being bullied at school, would you …
  a tell him or her to fight back?
  b go with your friend to report it to the headteacher?
  c say nothing and just hope it would stop?

4 If you found a purse or a wallet in the street, would you take it straight to a police station?
  a Yes, I would.
  b No, I wouldn't. I'd look inside to see if there was a name and address and if not, I'd keep it.
  c I'd take it to the nearest shop and leave it with the shopkeeper.

5 If I won some prize money to spend on my local community, …
  a I'd have a party for everybody in my block or my street.
  b I'd plant lots of flowers to make the area look nicer.
  c I'd ask people who didn't have much money what they needed.

Speaking

2 Work with a partner. Compare your answers. If you disagree, explain why.

A *If I was sitting on a bus and I saw several old people standing, I'd stand up and give one of them my seat.*

B *I wouldn't because they might not be very old and they might be quite happy to stand.*

Listening 25

3 Listen. What do the people talking have in common?

4 Listen again. For each person, answer these questions:

- Where do they live?
- What's their project?
- What do people say?

1 George
2 Chanelle
3 Sonia and Brandon

These schoolchildren in San Juan del Sur in Nicaragua painted a mural to make their local area look better.

Project: How to improve your local area

5 Work in groups. Imagine you won a lot of money to improve your local area. What would you do?

- Discuss your ideas.
- Choose one of your ideas. Write a short paragraph saying what you would do and why.

  We would create more parks where children could play. There isn't enough open space in our area. We would build an adventure playground and we'd ask children to paint a big, colourful mural near the playgound.

- Present your ideas to the rest of the class. Use photos and drawings to illustrate your presentation. At the end of your presentation, ask if anyone has any questions.

  If we won a lot of money, we would …
  Here's a picture of what it would look like.

- As a class, vote for the three best ideas for improving your local area.

Poetry

1 **Which of these statements describe you?**

1 I enjoy reading stories about imaginary places and people.
2 I like using my imagination to write stories.
3 I like writing stories about things that actually happened.
4 I've got a good memory for facts.
5 When I read a description of a scene in a story, I can see a picture of it in my head.
6 I'm not good at making up stories.
7 I sometimes find it hard to concentrate at school. I often find myself thinking of other things – daydreaming – in lessons.

2 **Read the poem. Why is it called *In Daylight Strange*?**

3 **What happens in the poem? Answer these questions.**

1 Where does it take place?
2 Who is talking?
3 What does this person see?
4 Do the other people see what he sees? How do you know?
5 Who is Miss Wolfenden?
6 Look at the last two lines of the poem:

                                    … it was

   Because *I* thought of the lion, that the lion was there?
   What does this mean?

4 **Answer these questions.**

1 Which of these statements is true about *In Daylight Strange*?
   a The last word in a line rhymes with the last word in another line.
   b The sentences run over from one line into the next line.
   c The lines have a regular rhythm (like the ones in *Rain Falls Down* on page 100).
2 How does the style of the poem make it feel like a daydream?
3 If you had to illustrate this poem, what would you draw?

In Daylight Strange

It was last Friday at ten to four I
Thought of the lion walking into the playground.
I was sitting, thinking, at our table when
The thought of the lion simply came,
And the sun was very hot, and the lion
Was in the yard (in daylight strange, because
Lions go out at night). He was
An enormous, sudden lion and he
Appeared just like that and was crossing very
Slowly the dusty playground, looking
To neither side, coming towards the door. He was
Coloured a yellow that was nearly grey, or a
Grey that was nearly yellow. He was so
Quiet that only I could hear the huge feet
Solidly pacing, and at the playground door he
Stopped, and looked powerfully in. There was
A forest following him, out in the street,
And noises of parakeets. When he stopped,
Looking like a picture of a lion in the frame
Of the open door, his eyes looked on at
Everything inside with a stern, curious look, he
Didn't seem completely to understand. So
He waited a second or two before
He roared. All the reeds on the river bank
Trembled, a thousand feet
Scattered among the trees, birds rose in clouds
But no one jumped in the classroom, no one screamed,
No one ran to ring the firebell, and
Miss Wolfenden went on writing on the board.
It was just exactly as if
They hadn't heard at all, as if nobody had heard.
And yet I had heard, certainly,
Yes. I had heard,
And I didn't jump.
And would you say you were surprised? Because
You ought not to be surprised.
Why should I be frightened when it was
Because *I* thought of the lion, that the lion was there?

Alan Brownjohn

Note: In Britain, the school day usually finishes at 4 o'clock or before. Friday is the last day of the school week.

pacing walking with regular steps around a small area
parakeets small, brightly-coloured parrots
stern strict and severe
roared made a long, deep noise
reeds tall thin plants that grow near water
trembled past tense of *tremble*, to shake because you are frightened or worried
scattered moved in different directions
rose past tense of *rise*, to go up

117

Review Units 13–14

Vocabulary

School

1 Find the verb for each definition.

1 talk about nothing important
2 want someone to believe they can do something
3 speak while someone else is speaking
4 take someone's attention away from something
5 give something all your attention

- interrupt
- distract
- chat
- concentrate
- encourage

In town

2 Write the names of the shops. You can buy …

1 bread at *the bakery*.
2 meat at the _____ .
3 flowers at the _____ .
4 newspapers and magazines at the _____ .
5 pens and paper at the _____ .
6 medicines at the _____ .
7 rings, watches, bracelets and necklaces at the _____ .

3 Decide whether these adjectives are positive or negative. Write two lists.

friendly	clean	crowded
dirty	exciting	boring
noisy	smoky	unfriendly
interesting		

positive: friendly, …
negative: …

4 Write three sentences about your town or city using at least three adjectives from Exercise 3.

Use of English

5 Complete the sentences using the prepositions and the verbs in the boxes.

by	for (x 2)		from	of (x 2)	on
ask	talk (x 2)	do	play	try	
get on with					

1 I can't concentrate *on doing* my homework when my little brother's in the room.
2 You shouldn't be scared _____ questions in class when you don't understand something.
3 At primary school I used to get into trouble _____ to my friends in class.
4 Seeing my friends playing outside distracts me _____ my work.
5 I never get tired _____ cricket!
6 Our teachers don't tell us off _____ if it's about the work we're doing.
7 I learn best _____ to do something for myself instead of someone showing me how to do it.

6 Choose the correct option.

1 We've decided (*to put / putting*) on a play at the end of term.
   We've decided <u>to put</u> on a play at the end of term.
2 I enjoy (*to do/ doing*) sports at school.
3 I hope (*to be / being*) in the athletics team next term.
4 Our teacher agreed (*to let / letting*) us have more time to work on our project.
5 I don't mind (*to play / playing*) football in the rain.
6 It's important to learn (*to make / making*) your own decisions.

7 Rewrite the sentences using the verbs in the box in the past simple. Use each verb once.

allow	not expect	ask
encourage	invite	

1 Mrs Santos: 'Marina, please would you put the books away?'

Mrs Santos asked Marina to put the books away.

2 My friend's parents: 'Would you like to go sailing on Saturday?'

3 My friend: 'You're early! Sorry, I'm not ready yet!'

4 The English teacher: 'You can use a dictionary in the test.'

5 The sports teacher: 'I think you should try the long jump. You'd be good at it.'

8 Complete the sentences with *have* + a suitable verb.

1 I can't see the blackboard. I need *to have* my eyes *tested*.

2 Your hair looks nice. Where do you _____ it _____ ?

3 My parents don't have time to go to the supermarket so they _____ the shopping _____ .

4 _____ you ever _____ your photo _____ by a professional photographer?

5 My dad loves Italian coffee. He _____ it _____ from Italy!

6 My grandmother is 60 next month. We're going _____ a special cake _____ for her.

9 Use the prompts to write sentences for these imaginary situations. Remember to use the past simple in one clause and *would* in the other clause.

1 If you (*find*) a gold ring in the street, what (*you / do*)?

If you found a gold ring in the street, what would you do?

2 Where (*you / go*) if you (*can*) travel anywhere in the world?

3 If you (*can*) change one thing about your school, what (*it / be*)?

4 If a friend (*tell*) me a secret, I (*not / tell*) anyone about it.

5 If I (*get*) 100% in a maths exam, I (*be*) very surprised.

6 We (*not / be*) bored in the holidays if we (*have*) an adventure playground in the park.

7 I (*cycle*) to school if there (*be*) a safe place to leave my bike.

General knowledge quiz

10 Work with a partner. Answer the questions.

1 Can you name eight school subjects?

2 What is an expert?

3 In which lessons do you do experiments?

4 Where is Summerhill School?

5 What do you call schools that follow the Summerhill model?

6 What is a majority vote?

7 Look at the symbols. What are the shops? What can you buy or have done there?

8 In which country is Taipei?

9 What's the word for a meal you take with you on a trip to the countryside?

10 What causes air pollution?

Settling America

- **Topics** The first European settlers; stories from the American West
- **Use of English** Abstract nouns; compound nouns; expressing the past (revision of present perfect, past simple and past continuous)

The first European settlers

- Who were the first Europeans to settle in America?

Reading

1 What does the picture below illustrate?

The early settlers

The first European settlers arrived in North America in the seventeenth century. At that time there were about 10 million indigenous inhabitants. There were hundreds of distinct nations and tribes speaking more than 200 languages.

In 1620, a group of people set sail from England on a ship called the *Mayflower*. There were 102 men, women and children and 25 to 30 crew members from England and Holland. They were escaping from religious persecution and wanted to live in a new world. They set off in September and they arrived 66 days later in Cape Cod on the eastern coast of America.

They established a community at Plymouth in Massachusetts. The local Wampanoag people helped the settlers by giving them food and by showing them how to grow corn, catch fish in the rivers and avoid poisonous plants.

The first winter was very hard and only half of the settlers lived to see their first spring in New England. In November 1621, they had a special meal to celebrate their first successful harvest. At that first 'Thanksgiving' meal there were 53 settlers and 90 Wampanoag. The American tradition of having a special meal at the end of November has continued ever since.

By 1770, more than two million people lived and worked in the 13 British colonies on the east coast of America, from Massachusetts in the north to Georgia in the south.

But the people in the colonies resented paying high taxes to the British government and on 4th July, 1776, the colonies declared independence from the Kingdom of Great Britain and called themselves the United States of America. This led to war and ultimately to the creation of a new nation. Eventually, in 1783 the colonies gained their independence from Britain.

Vocabulary

2 Find a word in the text which means:

1 People who move to a new place where there were not many people before.
2 Groups of people who live together and share the same culture and language.
3 Began a journey by sea.
4 The people who work together on a ship.
5 Treating someone unfairly or cruelly because of their race, religion or belief.
6 Started a journey.
7 Containing a substance that can kill you, or make you very ill, if you eat or drink it.
8 Felt angry and upset about something that someone has done.
9 Money that you have to pay to the government.
10 When a country has its own government and is not controlled by another country.

3 Summarise the text by completing the timeline.

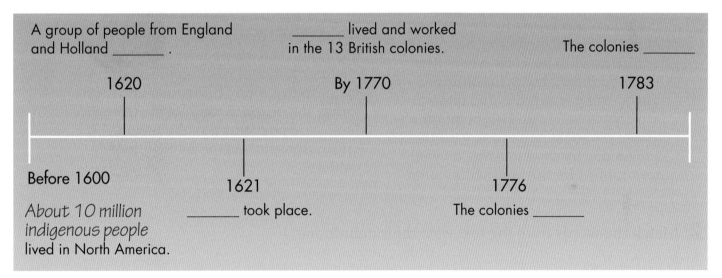

A group of people from England and Holland _____ .

_____ lived and worked in the 13 British colonies.

The colonies _____

1620   By 1770   1783

Before 1600

About 10 million indigenous people lived in North America.

1621   _____ took place.

1776   The colonies _____

4 Answer the questions.

1 How many people were living in North America when the first European settlers arrived?
2 What was the *Mayflower*?
3 Who travelled to America in 1620? Why?
4 Where did the first settlers establish their colony?
5 Did the first settlers get on well with the Wampanoag? How do you know?
6 Why did the first Thanksgiving meal take place?
7 Why were there only 53 settlers at the first Thanksgiving meal?
8 Who was at war between 1776 and 1783? Why?

The pioneers

- A pioneer is someone who is one of the first people to do something. Can you think of any pioneers?

Reading

1 Read the text. Who were the pioneer families?

In the mid-nineteenth century, about 400,000 people travelled west to find new land for farming. Life on the Pacific Coast meant opportunity. These pioneers joined other travellers and formed wagon trains to help each other travel along the Oregon Trail, a 2,000 mile route across the Great Plains and over the Rocky Mountains. The charity they showed others frequently meant the difference between life and death. Many pioneers died from accidents or disease, but hope for a new life inspired the pioneers to continue. The journey was hard, and often took between six and eight months. These pioneers had to carry all their provisions for their journey, as well as supplies for the new settlements in their wagons. When they finally arrived in Oregon, most spent their first winter clearing land and building log cabins. Gradually they built farms and schools, and their efforts resulted in whole towns and communities.

The first transcontinental railroad was finished in 1869, meaning that travellers could pass from the east coast to the west coast in as little as seven days. Use of the Oregon Trail declined, as it was easier, faster, and cheaper to travel west on the steam train. Today, many highways and roads follow the original route of the Oregon Trail, and pass through the towns originally established by the pioneer settlers.

2 Match the words from the text with their definitions.

1 b

1	opportunity	a	became less
2	charity	b	chance to do something
3	frequently	c	food you take with you on a journey
4	disease	d	food, clothes and the things you need in daily life, especially for a group of people
5	provisions		
6	supplies	e	illness, especially one that can be caused by infection
7	declined	f	kindness that you show to other people
		g	often

Writing

3 Write questions for these answers.

1 Q: *Why did the pioneer families travel west?*
A: To find land for farming.

2 Q: _____
A: They were groups of wagons travelling together.

3 Q: _____
A: It was a route to the Pacific Coast.

4 Q: _____
A: Six to eight months.

5 Q: _____
A: Provisions for the journey and supplies for the settlements.

6 Q: _____
A: No, they didn't. Many died from accidents and disease.

7 Q: _____
A: Clearing land and building log cabins.

8 Q: _____
A: It was finished in 1869.

9 Q: _____
A: It was faster, easier and cheaper.

10 Q: _____
A: Yes, you can, because many highways and roads follow the original route.

Use of English: Abstract nouns

Words like *independence* and *hope* are abstract nouns.

We usually use abstract nouns without *the* or *a*:
Life on the Pacific Coast meant opportunity.
NOT
~~The~~ *life on the Pacific Coast meant* ~~the~~ *opportunity.*

However, when you make an abstract noun specific rather than general, you need *the*:

The charity they showed others frequently meant the difference between life and death.

4 Give your opinion by choosing an abstract noun to complete the sentences. Remember to use *the* where necessary.

education	freedom	happiness	friendship
success	power	hope	peace
relaxation	wealth	health	

1 The most important thing in life is _____ .
2 _____ brings responsibility.
3 A school should be judged by _____ of its students.
4 _____ and _____ are important for a good life.
5 When people have no _____ they feel despair.
6 When you live in a city, you really notice _____ that surrounds you when you go to the country.

Speaking

5 Compare your sentences in small groups. Give reasons for your opinions like this:

A: *The most important thing in life is education, because it helps you to understand the world and to get a good job.*

B: *I don't agree. I think the most important thing in life is … because …*

Going west

- What is a journal? Who might want to keep a journal and why?

Reading

1 Take 20 seconds to look at the extract from *Rachel's Journal*.
When was the journal written? What does it describe?

Rachel's *Journal*

Uncle Pete has described tall, tall trees and high snowy mountains. He says California is the most beautiful place in the world. We might even see a grizzly bear.

April 12, 1850
We have been on the road for more than a month, and we still have not left the States. I did not realize how big this country is! We have reached St Joseph, Missouri, where we are to meet some neighbors to form a train together. I am sure I do not know how we will ever find them – white wagon covers stretch for miles. There are so many people and cattle waiting for the ferry to cross the Missouri River and start on the Oregon Trail, it seems our time will never come.

July 12, 1850
While we were at supper a boy walked into camp. He had all his belongings with him, loaded onto a cow. His name is Simon and he walked all the way from Ohio by himself. Sometimes he camped with nearby emigrants, but mostly he has been alone. Mother was horrified that one so young should be by himself in this great wilderness – he cannot be more than 12. Of course, we fed him supper (which he bolted like a famished dog), and after some hurried whispers from Mother to Pa, and from Pa to Mr Bridger, Mr Bridger invited Simon to join his

wagon. Simon can drive the team in exchange for his food. Simon does not smile much, but I think he is glad of the company. Mr Bridger, naturally, is delighted – one fewer task to keep him from napping.

September 30, 1850
We traveled all night through a nightmare landscape. Lee and Daniel led the way with lanterns, but the moon was bright enough to show us the dead cattle, horses, and mules strewn everywhere, along with objects left behind by desperate emigrants. There were whole wagons, trunks, furniture, bedding, tools, a catalogue of goods. Emma and I went on a treasure hunt, pretending we were exploring sunken pirate ships on the sandy sea bottom.

October 23, 1850
This morning we woke up early. The guidebook showed that there were only a dozen or so miles ahead, and no one wanted to sleep. We descended the last stretch of eight miles. The road is smooth and level, dotted with farms and homesteads. We are finally safely here.

2 Read the text and answer the questions.

1 Who is Rachel?
2 How old do you think she is?
3 Who is she travelling with?
4 Where is Rachel when she writes the diary entry for 12 April?

5 Where are Rachel and her family going?
6 Why do you think they're going there?
7 Who is Simon?
8 Who is Mr Bridger?

3 Match these descriptions to the tenses in the *Use of English* box.

1 Use this for an action completed in the past.
2 Use this for a situation continuing up to now.
3 Use this for an action in progress in the past.

Listening 26

4 Listen to another story from the wagon train. Is the girl happy about what happened? Why?

5 Complete the sentences to make a summary of the story. Remember to use the correct tense: present perfect, past simple or past continuous.

1 We *'ve been* with the wagon train for six weeks now.
2 People have told us scary stories but we _____ any problems yet.
3 Yesterday, while we _____ for wood for the campfire, a young boy suddenly _____ .
4 He smiled and he _____ to us in English.
5 He _____ one of our young cows in exchange for a horse.
6 The boy was so pleased that he also _____ me a beautiful bracelet and a necklace.

Use of English: Expressing the past – revision

You need to use the correct tense when talking about the past.

Present perfect

We have been on the road for more than a month.
We still have not left the States.

Past simple

We fed him supper.
Mr Bridger invited Simon to join his wagon.

Past continuous

(We were) pretending we were exploring sunken pirate ships.

Project: A diary entry

6 Imagine you're on a wagon train in the 1850s. Write a diary entry like the one you've just heard.

● First answer these questions:
1 How long have you been on the wagon train?
2 Who are you travelling with?
3 How has the journey been so far?
● Then write a draft of your story.
  We've been with the wagon train for …
● Show your story to another student. Check each other's stories for mistakes.
● Write a final version of your story.
● Read your story to the class.

- **Topics** The Silk Road; a traditional story from Uzbekistan
- **Use of English** Participles used as adjectives; *so* and *such* to add emphasis

From East to West

- How many materials for clothes can you think of? Where do they come from?

Reading

1 Look at the map and read the captions from right to left. What does the map show?

2 Look at the map and answer the questions.
1 Where did the Silk Road start?
2 What time of year did the journey start?
3 What kind of animals did people use to carry the silk?
4 What's the word for a group of people with animals who travel together for safety?
5 What animals did the Chinese buy to take back to China?
6 What did the travellers find in the oasis city of Kashgar?
7 What goods did the private merchants find in Tashkent and Herat?
8 How did the silk get from Tyre to Byzantium?

Did you know?

The Silk Road was a trade route between East and West from about 2000 BCE until the fourteenth century. It brought together people from many different countries and cultures and was a link between East and West for over 3000 years. It wasn't only important for trading goods – ideas about astronomy, medicine and art also travelled along the Silk Road.

What is special about silk?

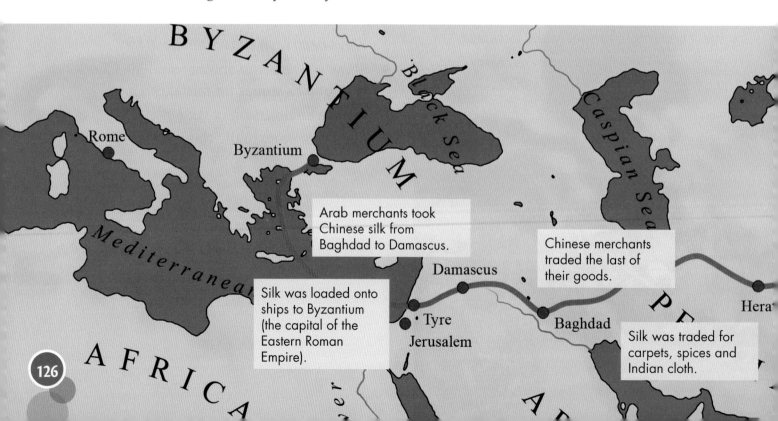

Arab merchants took Chinese silk from Baghdad to Damascus.

Chinese merchants traded the last of their goods.

Silk was loaded onto ships to Byzantium (the capital of the Eastern Roman Empire).

Silk was traded for carpets, spices and Indian cloth.

Listening 27

3 Listen and follow the Silk Road on the map.
Point to the places on the map as they are mentioned.

4 Listen again. What can you say about the following?

1 Chang'an
2 The reason for starting the Silk Road journey in spring
3 The journey from Dunhuang across the Taklamakan Desert
4 Kashgar

5 Tashkent
6 The people the Chinese merchants met in Herat
7 Baghdad
8 Tyre
9 Byzantium

Speaking

5 Divide the class into groups. Take one section of the Silk Road each and describe the journey from East to West. You can listen again to help you.

The journey of the Silk Road started in Chang'an, the capital of China and the largest city in the world at that time …

6 Discuss these questions.

- Is silk exported from China today?
- What else is exported from China?
- What is exported from your country?

- What is imported?
- How are these things moved from one country to another?

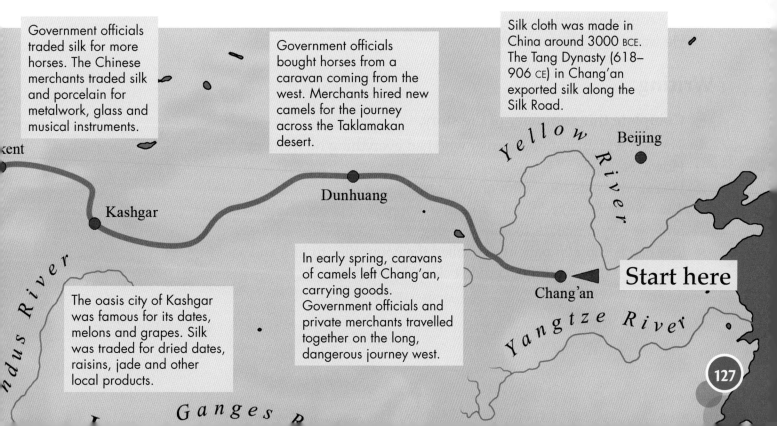

Government officials traded silk for more horses. The Chinese merchants traded silk and porcelain for metalwork, glass and musical instruments.

Government officials bought horses from a caravan coming from the west. Merchants hired new camels for the journey across the Taklamakan desert.

Silk cloth was made in China around 3000 BCE. The Tang Dynasty (618–906 CE) in Chang'an exported silk along the Silk Road.

In early spring, caravans of camels left Chang'an, carrying goods. Government officials and private merchants travelled together on the long, dangerous journey west.

The oasis city of Kashgar was famous for its dates, melons and grapes. Silk was traded for dried dates, raisins, jade and other local products.

Kashgar

Dunhuang

Beijing

Yellow River

Chang'an

Start here

Yangtze River

Indus River

Ganges R

127

A Rainbow in Silk: Part 1

- This is the first part of a traditional story from Uzbekistan. The capital of Uzbekistan is Tashkent. Can you find it on the Silk Road map on pages 126 and 127?

Reading

1 Read the story and look at the illustration. What does each part of the illustration show?

Vocabulary

2 How many adjectives and adverbs can you find in the story? Make two lists. Which are positive and which are negative?

3 Use the prompts to complete the sentences with the correct adjective.

1 (interest)
The Beg was wasn't *interested*.
The new carpet wasn't _____ .
2 (amaze)
The blue glass swan was _____ .
Everyone in the court was _____ when they saw it.
3 (frighten)
The counsellor was so _____ that he couldn't sleep.
It was a _____ thought.
4 (excite)
The counsellor had an _____ idea.
He was _____ beyond belief.

> **Use of English: Participles used as adjectives**
>
> We can use present participles and past participles as adjectives. It's important to know the difference.
>
> The Beg was bored. (past participle)
> Life was boring. (present participle)

Writing

4 Complete this summary of the story.

1 The Beg was an important ruler who had everything he wanted. However, …
2 He called for his counsellor and said that …
3 The counsellor asked the doctors, the writers and poets, the glassblower and the carpet makers to help. The Beg …
4 The Beg became impatient. He called the counsellor to him and said …
5 That night the counsellor couldn't sleep. However, …

There was once a Beg – an important ruler – who had everything that any man could have wanted. He rode about the city on a magnificent white horse and admired its orchards and gardens, and the fine mosques whose domes gleamed blue and turquoise in the morning sun. The treasuries were full, the harvests were good, the Beg had no foreign enemies to worry about. But the Beg was very, very bored.

One day he could stand it no longer. He sent for his adviser, a man who had served him well for many years.

'I want something new!' he said, and tears came to his eyes like a spoilt child. 'I'm bored! There's nothing to do any more!'

His counsellor was horrified. He had never had to deal with a situation like this before. He scratched his chin anxiously. 'Well,' he said miserably, 'I really don't know, Your Nobleness.'

'Then think of something!' the Beg hissed, and turned away. The counsellor bowed, then retreated thankfully. What had got into his master? Straight away he summoned all the best artists and craftsmen in the town, all the writers and poets, all the tumblers and clowns, all the star-gazers and doctors, and asked their advice.

The doctors gave him potions which they said were recipes for Eternal Life.

'Hah! Eternal Life! Well, I shan't know, shall I? Not till you're dead and gone!' And he gave the doctors such a nasty look that they hurried away.

The writers and poets scribbled furiously and begged to be allowed to read their new works to the Beg. But he yawned loudly whenever they tried.

Everybody was losing patience with the Beg, but of course they didn't dare show it.

The glass-blower brought a swan which he had made of fine blue glass. Everyone in the court gasped as he carried it in, it was so beautiful. The Beg reached out to snatch it and smash it, but the glass-blower managed to keep it just out of his reach.

The carpet weavers worked day and night in teams to complete a fine and huge carpet showing the Beg on his favourite horse. But the Beg wasn't interested.

Finally, he summoned his adviser again. 'You've got one more day!' he roared at him. 'Don't you understand? I'M BORED! I want something new! By tomorrow! Or else!'

The counsellor was terrified.

The night wore on, and the poor counsellor didn't sleep at all.

At last the first rays of the morning sun crept through his window. The counsellor's eyes were wet with tears. And as the light touched the teardrops on his eyelashes, suddenly a brilliant rainbow appeared before his eyes.

'That's it!' He sat up in bed, excited beyond belief.

He ran into the Beg's presence and knelt down before him. 'Your Highness, I think I can do it! I have a wonderful idea! Just give me a few more days.'

Even the Beg could see that the counsellor was excited. The Beg nodded graciously and dismissed him.

Adapted from *A Rainbow in Silk, Stories from the Silk Road* by Cherry Gilchrist, Barefoot Books, 1999

A Rainbow in Silk: Part 2

- What can you remember about the first part of the story,
  A Rainbow in Silk?

Speaking

1 Work with a partner. Ask and answer these questions.

1 Q: Who was the Beg?
   A: *He was an important ruler.*
2 Why was the Beg unhappy?
3 What was the counsellor's first reaction?
4 What did the counsellor do first?
5 What did the doctors do? What was the Beg's reaction?
6 What did the writers and poets do? What was the Beg's reaction?
7 What did the glass-blower and the carpet weavers do? What was the
   Beg's reaction?
8 What did the Beg do when he'd seen everything that people
   had brought him?
9 Why couldn't the counsellor sleep?
10 What gave the counsellor an idea?

Use of English: *so* and *such*

We use *so* and *such* to add emphasis:

so   adjective   I'm *so* bored!
such   (adjective +) noun   It was *such* an amazing sight.

Both can be followed by a clause beginning with *that*:

*The glass swan was so beautiful that everyone in the court was amazed
when they saw it.*
He gave the doctors such a nasty look that they hurried away.

Remember to use *a / an* before singular countable nouns: *such a bad
mood, such a beautiful sight.*

You can also add emphasis to adverbs by using *so*:
… shining so brightly in the morning sun.

---

2 Put *so* or *such (a / an)* in these sentences.

1 It was *such a* beautiful city.
2 'This is _____ wonderful potion,' said the doctors.
3 'These poems are _____ silly,' said the Beg.
4 The carpet weavers worked _____ hard to finish their carpet.
5 'This is _____ waste of time,' said the Beg.

3 Combine these sentences using *so … that,* or *such … that.*

1 The city was beautiful. People came from far away to see it.

The city was so beautiful that people came from far away to see it.

2 The Beg was rich. He could have anything he wanted.

3 The counsellor was worried. He asked everyone in the city to help him.

4 It was a beautiful swan. Everyone was amazed.

5 The Beg was a difficult man. No one knew what to do.

Project: Creative writing

4 How do you think the story ends? Work in groups.

● Ask everyone in your group for their ideas and write them down.

● Choose the best ideas and use them to write the ending of the story.

● Ask your teacher to check your work.

● Make any corrections necessary.

● Read your version of the ending to the rest of the class.

Listening 28

5 Listen to the original ending of the story. Is it similar to yours?

6 Listen again and answer the questions.

1 Why did the counsellor ask the silk weavers and the dyers (people who add colour to material) to help him?

2 What did the Beg think of the counsellor's gift?

3 How is this story connected to people today?

7 Which ending to the story did you like best, yours or the original one? Why?

> **Language tip**
>
> Remember to use the past perfect when you're already talking about the past and you want to talk about an earlier past.
>
> *The counsellor had served him well for many years.*

Fiction

Akbar and Birbal

There are many stories from India about the Emperor Akbar and his trusted adviser Birbal. They are based on a real emperor, Akbar the Great (1542–1605), and his favourite counsellor, Birbal.

1 **Answer the following questions.**

1 What do the following have in common: king, queen, emperor, empress, tsar, tsarina, president?

2 Can you think of examples from history or from today for each of the people in question 1?

3 Do all rulers need counsellors (people who give them advice)? Why?

2 **Read the two stories. What do they have in common?**

A Journey

The Emperor Akbar was travelling to a city a long way from his home. It was hot and he was beginning to feel tired and bored.

"Can anybody shorten this road for me?" he asked impatiently.

The courtiers looked at one another anxiously. They knew there was no shorter road through the mountains to their destination.

"I can," said Birbal.

"You can shorten the road?" said the emperor. "Well, go on, do it!"

"I will," said Birbal. "But first listen to this story."

Birbal rode beside the emperor and began to tell a story. It was a very exciting tale, full of adventure and mystery. All the listeners were fascinated. Before they knew it, they had reached the end of their journey.

"We've arrived!" exclaimed Akbar. "So soon!"

"Well," smiled Birbal, "you did say you wanted the road to be shortened."

The Chicken or the Egg?

One day a man came to the court of Emperor Akbar to challenge Birbal. He'd heard stories about how clever Birbal was and he wanted him to prove it.

The man approached Birbal. "Would you prefer to answer a hundred easy questions or just one difficult question?" he asked.

Both the emperor and Birbal had had a difficult day. They were tired and they wanted to go home.

"Ask me one difficult question," said Birbal.

"Well then, tell me," said the man, "which came first into the world, the chicken or the egg?"

"The chicken," replied Birbal.

"How do you know?" asked the man, thinking he had trapped Birbal.

"We had agreed you would ask only one question and you have already asked it," said Birbal. He and the emperor walked away, leaving the man speechless.

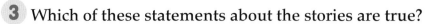

3 Which of these statements about the stories are true?

1 The writer starts by describing in detail the place and the time.
2 The stories are mainly based on dialogue.
3 The stories contain a lot of description.
4 The paragraphs are short.
5 You don't know exactly how the story will end until you get to the last paragraph.

4 Read the *The Mango Tree*. How do you think Birbal settled the argument? Write the final paragraph.

The Mango Tree

Two men, Ram and Sham, were having an argument about a mango tree. "It's mine," said Ram. "No," said Sham, "it belongs to me."

They asked Birbal to settle the argument.

"There is only one way to settle this," said Birbal. "Pick all the fruit from the tree and divide it equally between you. Then cut down the tree and divide the wood."

Ram thought this was fair. But Sham was horrified.

"With respect, sir," said Sham, "I've looked after that tree for seven years. I'd rather let Ram have it than cut it down."

5 Work in groups. Read your final paragraph to the other members of your group and listen to their final paragraphs. Can you improve what you have written?

133

Review of Units 15–16

Vocabulary

Settling America

1 Complete the text using the words in the box.

crops	disease	harvest
independent	people	log cabins
poisonous	set sail	pioneers
tradition	wagon trains	

A group of *pioneers*[1] from England and Holland _____[2] in a ship called the *Mayflower* and reached Cape Cod in 1620. The indigenous _____[3] helped them to grow _____[4], catch fish and avoid eating _____[5] plants.

The following year, the settlers had a special 'Thanksgiving' meal to celebrate their first _____[6] in America. The _____[7] of having a special meal at the end of November has continued since that time.

In 1783, the British colonies in North America became _____[8]. In the years that followed, many people went west to find land. They travelled in _____[9]. Many pioneers died from _____[10].

When the travellers reached the west, some cleared land for farming and built _____[11] to live in. They built towns and schools too.

The Silk Road

2 Match the words to the definitions.

silk	merchant	hire	trade
porcelain	jade		export	counsellor

People

1 someone who gives advice   *counsellor*
2 someone who buys and sells things in large quantities

Goods

3 a fine white substance used to make plates and cups
4 a type of cloth which is soft and smooth
5 a stone, usually green, which is used to make jewellery

Verbs to do with buying and selling

6 to buy and sell goods
7 to pay money to borrow or use something for a time
8 to sell things to another country

Use of English

3 Make adjectives from these nouns using the suffixes *-ful*, *-ous* or *-y*.
(A suffix is a letter or letters you add to the end of a word to make a new word.)

1 beauty   *beautiful*   5 danger
2 poison   6 sand
3 snow   7 wonder
4 success   8 religion

4 Make abstract nouns from these adjectives to complete the sentences.

happy	independent	peaceful
free	powerful	

1 November 1621 was a time of great *happiness* for the settlers because there had been a good harvest.
2 In 1783, the American colonies gained their _____ from Britain.
3 The people in the American colonies resented the _____ the British had over them.
4 No-one wants war. Everyone wants to live in _____ .
5 The European settlers went to America, so that they could have the _____ to live as they wanted to.

5 Where do you need to use *the* in the following text? For each numbered gap, write – or *the*.   *1 –*

Today people move from one country to another to escape _____¹ poverty and, in some cases, _____² persecution. They hope to find _____³ work, a place to live and _____⁴ happiness. For some emigrants, moving to a new country brings _____⁵ success. But then there is _____⁶ despair that others feel when they can't find a job or a place to live. They miss _____⁷ friendship of people back home and begin to wish that they had never left.

6 Complete the diary of a journey using the correct tense: past simple, past perfect or past continuous.

Diary of a journey

Day 1

We (set) *have set*¹ sail at last! As we (leave) *were leaving*² the harbour, the sun (come) *came*³ out from behind the clouds. The wind was light and the sea was calm.

This afternoon, while I (read) _____⁴ in the cabin, my brother suddenly (shout) _____⁵, "Come quickly! Dolphins!" But I (be) _____⁶ too late. I ran up to the deck but the dolphins (go) _____⁷ before I got there.

It's now 8 o'clock. We (have) _____⁸ our first day at sea and I'm ready for bed.

Day 2

There was a big storm this morning. It (begin) _____⁹ at about 8 o'clock while we (have) _____¹⁰ our breakfast. My brother and I (go) _____¹¹ down into the cabin and we (stay) _____¹² there until the storm was over. It (not last) _____¹³ long, but it was quite frightening.

It's now 5 o'clock and I (be) _____¹⁴ here on deck all afternoon watching for dolphins. But I (not see) _____¹⁵ any. Maybe tomorrow!

7 Choose the correct adjective for each sentence.

1 I never get *bored / boring*. I can always find something to do.

I never get bored. I can always find something to do.

2 We're going to Canada on holiday. I'm so *excited / exciting*.

3 Learning about history isn't *bored / boring*.

4 I'm *interested / interesting* in music.

5 The book was good, but the film was *disappointed / disappointing*.

6 I'm *frightened / frightening* of snakes and spiders.

7 The pyramids in Mexico are *amazed / amazing*.

8 Find the sentences which match. Join them by using *so … that* or *such a … that*.

1 g The film was so boring that I fell asleep for half an hour.

1 The film was boring.
2 I've been very busy.
3 We had a really good holiday.
4 The sea was clear and blue.
5 The book was exciting.
6 It was a wonderful day.
7 It was a difficult exam.

a We decided to go for a picnic.
b I couldn't put it down.
c I haven't had time for lunch.
d Nobody passed.
e We wanted to swim in it all day.
f I fell asleep for half an hour.
g We're planning to go to the same place next year.

Festivals around the world

- **Topics** Festivals
- **Use of English** Prepositional phrases, compound adjectives

Happy New Year!

- Why do people celebrate New Year?

Reading

1 Find a sentence in the text to use as a caption for the photo on page 137.

Chinese New Year is the most important celebration in the Chinese calendar. It is also known as the spring festival because it celebrates the start of new life and the season for planting crops. It is the oldest Chinese festival.

New Year festivities start when the moon is new, on the first day of the lunar month in the Chinese calendar, in January or February (between 21st January and 20th February). Celebrations continue until the fifteenth day, when the moon is brightest.

Just before New Year, people clean their houses. They decorate them with pieces of paper with words such as 'Happiness' and 'Wealth' written on them. On New Year's Eve, families get together and have a special meal. People dress in red, which symbolises fire, and set off fireworks.

At the start of the first week of New Year, people visit friends and family. The second week ends with the Lantern Festival on the fifteenth day of the month. People light lanterns to put in the windows of their houses. They walk in the streets carrying them under the light of the full moon.

One of the highlights of the Chinese New Year is the dragon dance. The dragons are made of paper, silk and bamboo. Chinese people think of dragons as helpful, friendly creatures which symbolise long life and wisdom.

Vocabulary

2 Match the words from the text to the definitions.

1	crops	a	an imaginary creature that breathes fire
2	festivities	b	a light that can be carried
3	lunar	c	celebrations at a festival
4	fireworks	d	connected with the moon
5	lantern	e	good sense and judgement based on experience
6	dragon	f	plants like rice, corn or vegetables grown by farmers
7	wisdom	g	containers filled with powder that you light to produce a bang or bright colours

3 What is the connection between Chinese New Year and the following?

1 spring   *Spring is the start of new life in the new year.*

2 the moon
3 cleaning the house
4 the colour red

5 fireworks
6 lanterns
7 dragons

Speaking

4 Work with a partner. Ask and answer questions about Chinese New Year:

When does Chinese New Year start?

Listening 29

5 Listen to this description of New Year. Which country is it about? Which traditions are similar to Chinese New Year?

6 Listen again and complete the summary.

On New Year's Eve, people *clean the house*[1] and they wear _____[2]. They light candles and _____[3]. On a piece of paper, they _____[4]; on another piece they _____[5]. The family gets together for _____[6]. They eat _____[7]. At midnight, they eat _____[8] and make a wish each time. They read out their _____[9]; they burn the other piece of paper. After midnight, they throw _____[10]. This symbolises throwing out the bad things from the old year.

Use of English: Prepositional time phrases

Remember to use the correct prepositions in expressions of time.

in January	at the start of the
on the first day of	first week
the lunar month	at New Year
on New Year's Eve	at midnight

Write the correct preposition to complete the rules.

Use _____ with months, years, seasons
Use _____ with days, dates
Use _____ with clock times, festivals and 'the weekend'

Notice that we say:
'on Monday morning' but 'in the morning'.

Writing

7 Write about how you and your family celebrate New Year.

● Use these questions as a guide.
1 When do you celebrate New Year?
2 What happens on New Year's Eve?
3 What does your family do at New Year? Who has a party?
4 Who do you like to spend New Year with?
● Include the traditions that you share with the Chinese New Year or New Year in Cuba.
● Remember to use the correct prepositions in time expressions.

Three festivals

● Name a festival. What does it celebrate?

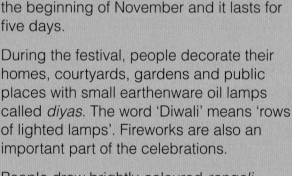

Diwali

Reading

1 Read about Diwali, Eid al-Fitr and Maslenitsa. Then copy and complete the chart.

Festival, religion (country)	When?	How long?	Key features
Diwali, Hindu			
Eid al-Fitr, Islam			
Maslenitsa, Christian (Russia)			

Diwali is the 'festival of lights' which celebrates the Hindu New Year. It is an important holiday in India and it is celebrated by communities around the world. The festival takes place at the end of October or the beginning of November and it lasts for five days.

During the festival, people decorate their homes, courtyards, gardens and public places with small earthenware oil lamps called *diyas*. The word 'Diwali' means 'rows of lighted lamps'. Fireworks are also an important part of the celebrations.

People draw brightly-coloured *rangoli* patterns on the floor near the entrance to their houses and light many *diyas*.

Rangoli a traditional Indian decoration made from coloured rice, sand or flower petals.

Speaking

2 Work with a partner. Using the information in the chart in Exercise 1, take turns to ask and answer questions about the festivals.

A *When does Diwali take place?*
B *At the end of October or the beginning of November.*

3 Read the texts again. With your partner, write five more questions. Then ask other students to answer them.

Where is Diwali an important holiday?

Vocabulary

4 Which of these words are nouns and which are verbs? Write two lists. (One word can go in both lists.)

- celebration
- festival
- festivities
- decorate
- fireworks
- lantern
- symbol
- dance
- candle
- celebrate
- decoration
- symbolise
- bonfire
- represent

Eid al-Fitr

Eid al-Fitr celebrates the end of Ramadan in the Islamic world. Ramadan is the ninth month of the Islamic calendar. It's a time of fasting – going without food or drink during the day. The festival of Eid begins when the new moon is first seen in the sky.

Eid lasts for one, two or three days. The day starts with a small breakfast before going to prayers in open areas or at the mosque. After prayers, people visit their family and friends. Then there are special meals which may include meat, vegetable and rice dishes. There are usually a lot of sweet dishes, such as home-made halva and ice cream.

Use of English: Compound adjectives

You can use two words together to make a compound adjective:

brightly-coloured rangoli patterns

5 Find four more compound adjectives in the descriptions of the festivals.

Writing

6 Write about a festival in your country as if you are describing it to an English-speaking friend. Use the texts as a model. Say what you like best about the festival.

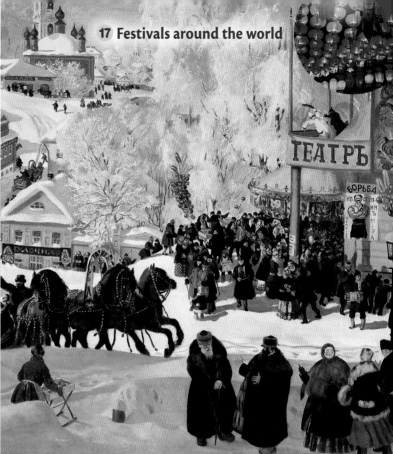

Maslenitsa

The Russian festival of Maslenitsa takes place in February or March and lasts a week. It's a time to say goodbye to winter and to welcome the spring. At the beginning of the week, children make a large doll from straw and old clothes. This is Lady Maslenitsa, representing winter. The painting shows Maslenitsa a hundred years ago, with horse-drawn sleighs, snow-covered streets and people dressed in warm, fur-lined coats.

Today, Maslenitsa is still a time for having fun, and for eating *blinis*. These are pancakes, made from eggs, butter and milk and served with butter, cream, jam, honey or caviar. Some people say they are a symbol of the sun, giving the earth warmth.

Maslenitsa also comes just before the period of Lent, when Christians traditionally give up rich foods.

At the end of the week, the straw doll is burnt on a bonfire. Winter is over and spring is on the way.

April Fools' Day

- Is it OK to play jokes on people?

Reading

1 Look at the photo. What does it show?

2 Read the text and answer these questions.

1 What does this story tell you about what happens on 1st April in Britain?

2 What do you think the BBC said to the people who phoned to ask about spaghetti plants?

Listening 30

3 Here is a list of some of the things people do on April Fools' Day or on a similar day. Listen. Which countries are mentioned? Make a list.

4 Listen again. Match the activities with the countries.

- **a** putting a picture of a fish on someone's back
- **b** having a picnic
- **c** dancing and singing
- **d** throwing flour over people
- **e** in newspapers, printing stories that aren't true
- **f** throwing coloured water
- **g** having a bonfire
- **h** playing games
- **i** telling jokes

On 1st April 1957, there was a programme on British TV which featured a family in Ticino in Switzerland harvesting spaghetti from trees and putting it in the sun to dry. At that time, not many people in Britain had eaten spaghetti, so they didn't know much about it. They phoned the BBC* to ask where they could buy spaghetti plants. They hadn't realised that it was 1st April, April Fools' Day.

* BBC = British Broadcasting Corporation

Did you know?

The tradition of playing jokes on people and having fun at the beginning of spring comes from Persia and from Ancient Rome. Persia, now Iran, has the oldest known fun day, dating back to 536 BCE.

Is there a day in your country which is a 'fun' day? What do people do?

If there isn't a fun day in your country, do you think there should be? Why?

Speaking

5 Work with a partner. Ask and answer about the fun days and festivals in Exercise 3. Listen again to help you remember the details.

A When do people in France have a fun day?
B It's usually on 1st April.

A What do they do?
B They …

Writing

6 Work in pairs. Write a newspaper story to appear on April Fools' Day.

- Think of some possible stories.
- Choose the best idea and write your story.
- You can start the story with one of the following phrases:

Scientists have invented a …

The government has decided to …

Starting next term, all schools will …

Experts have discovered a new kind of animal in …

On TV tonight there's a programme about …

During a football match last night, …

Project: An information poster about a festival

7 Make an information poster about one of the following festivals.

Songkran (Thailand)
The Moon Festival (China)

Carnival (Brazil, Italy, etc.)
Setsubun (Japan)

St John's Eve (Scandinavia)

Work in groups. Find the answers to these questions.
Use the Internet or other sources for your research.

1 When and where is it celebrated?
2 What does it celebrate?
3 How long does it last?
4 What happens during the festival?
5 What special events are there?
6 What do people eat during the festival?

Decide on the most important points to include on the poster.

- Who is going to design the poster?
- Who is going to find the pictures?
- Who is going to do the illustrations?

Make the poster. Then use it to give a presentation to the rest of the class.

18

Using English

- **Topics** The theatre; performing a play; the story of *Aladdin*
- **Use of English** *like* and *as* to say that things are similar; reported speech – commands

At the theatre

- Which do you think is more difficult: to be an actor in a film, or on stage in a play? Why?

Vocabulary and listening 31

1 Listen to this description of a visit to the theatre. Write the words for each of the numbered items in the picture.

- actor
- audience
- costume
- curtain
- orchestra
- props
- scenery
- stage

1 curtain

2 Work with a partner. Look at the picture and listen again. What can you say about the following?

- the scenery   *The scenery is quite simple, just …*
- the orchestra
- the costumes
- the props
- the audience

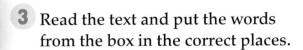

3 Read the text and put the words from the box in the correct places.

cast	performances
lines	play
main characters	rehearsals
make-up	scene
parts	script

I was in the school *play*[1]. One of the teachers wrote the _____[2].

There were fourteen students in the _____[3]: four _____[4] and ten minor _____[5]. I played one of the main characters.

We all had to wear stage _____[6] to make us look older and more dramatic. When I looked in the mirror, I hardly recognised myself!

I had a lot of _____[7] to learn. I had to go to all the _____[8] after school because I was in every _____[9].

We gave two _____[10], one for the other students and one for parents. It was a great success. The audiences really enjoyed the play, and so did we.

4 **(32)** Listen and check.

Speaking

5 Work in small groups. Ask and answer.

Have you ever been in a play?

Yes ← → No

Yes

1 What was the play?
2 What part did you play?
3 Were you one of the main characters?
4 Did you wear a costume? Did you wear make-up?
5 What did you have to do? Did you have to sing or dance?
6 Are you good at learning lines?
7 Do you enjoy being on stage or are you nervous?
8 How many rehearsals were there?
9 How many performances did you give?
10 Which would you rather be, an actor or a director? Give reasons for your answer.

No

1 Have you got a good memory? Would you be good at learning lines?
2 Are you confident or do you get nervous when you have to talk in front of other people?
3 Are you a good singer or dancer?
4 What practical and technical skills do you have that would be useful in a theatre (e.g. painting, doing stage lighting)?
5 If you were in a play, which of the following would you like to be? Give reasons for your answer.
   - a main character
   - a minor character
   - someone who helps with the scenery, lighting, costumes or make-up

Writing

6 If you answered 'Yes' to the question in Exercise 5, write an account of the play using your answers.
If you answered 'No', write a paragraph about what you would like to do if your teacher asked you to take part in a play.

The story of Aladdin: Part 1

- What sort of stories do you like? What makes a good story?

Reading

1 Read the first part of the story of Aladdin. Who are the main characters?

Once upon a time, there lived in a certain city in China a poor tailor who had a son called Aladdin. When Aladdin was ten, his father wanted to teach him to be a tailor, but Aladdin was lazy. He didn't like sewing and making clothes, so he ran off to play with his friends whenever his father tried to teach him.

Aladdin's father died, and his mother began spinning cotton to earn money. Aladdin carried on playing with his friends. One day, while he was playing in the street, a man saw Aladdin. "This is the boy I've been looking for," he said to himself.

"My boy!" he said to Aladdin. "At last I have found you!"

"Who are you?" asked Aladdin.

"I am your father's brother. I knew you were his son the moment I saw you. You're just like him."

"But my father is dead, sir," said Aladdin.

"Oh no!" said the man. "Then I am too late." And he began to cry. "Here, take these, my boy," he said, and gave Aladdin ten gold coins. "Give them to your mother and tell her that I should like to visit her tomorrow. Go now."

Aladdin ran like the wind and told his mother about the man. "He'd like to visit us tomorrow," he said.

"What are you talking about, Aladdin? Your father has no brothers living."

"But, mother, as I told you, he wants to come to see us tomorrow."

The man came to the house and told the story of how he had been away for many years and had wanted to see his brother again. He was heartbroken that he had arrived too late. Aladdin's mother was so moved by the man's tears that she believed his story. Neither she nor Aladdin realised that the man was in fact a sorcerer from Morocco.

The sorcerer offered to help Aladdin to become a merchant, selling silk in a shop of his own. Aladdin and his mother were delighted. He took Aladdin to the market and bought him a fine suit of clothes.

The following day, the sorcerer took Aladdin to a beautiful garden. In the garden, he showed Aladdin a big marble stone.

"Under that stone there is treasure that belongs to you, Aladdin. Come, lift the stone."

"But uncle," Aladdin replied, "I am not strong enough."

"Do as I say," said the sorcerer.

Aladdin used all his strength. The stone moved easily and Aladdin saw some steps down into a cave.

"Go down into the cave," said the sorcerer. "You will see all sorts of treasures. Keep going until you see a lamp. Bring back this lamp and you will be the richest man on earth. Here, this ring will help you if you are in danger. It will protect you. Don't lose it." He took a ring from his finger and gave it to Aladdin.

Aladdin went down into the cave, past the treasures and found the lamp. He took the lamp and on the way back to the opening of the cave, he helped himself to some of the treasure. But the entrance of the cave was so high that Aladdin could not climb out. "Help me, uncle!" he shouted.

"Give me the lamp first," the sorcerer replied.

"I cannot," replied Aladdin. "Just give me your hand to help me up, and then you can have the lamp."

The sorcerer became impatient and, thinking that Aladdin wanted to keep the lamp for himself, he made the marble stone move back into place by using a magic charm. Aladdin was imprisoned in the cave.

The sorcerer knew that the lamp would make the person who owned it the richest man on earth, but he was afraid that Aladdin would cheat him, so he made sure that he could not escape in order to use it.

Aladdin shouted and shouted, but no help came. At the end of three days without food or drink, he had given up hope when he happened to rub the ring that the sorcerer had given him. At once a genie appeared.

"I am here, master!" the genie said. "Your wish is my command."

Aladdin was terrified, but he remembered what the sorcerer had said about the ring.

"Take me back home," said Aladdin, and the next thing he knew he was back in the garden of his mother's house.

His mother cried with joy when she saw him. Aladdin now realised that the man who had given him the ring was not his uncle, but an evil sorcerer.

Vocabulary

2 Find these words in the extract. Try to work out their meaning from the context. If you're unsure, use a dictionary.

1 tailor 3 sorcerer 5 charm 7 rub
2 heartbroken 4 cave 6 cheat 8 genie

3 Answer these questions.

1 In which country is the story set? A second country is mentioned. Why?
2 What does this extract tell you about Aladdin's parents?
3 Aladdin met a man in the street. Who did the man pretend to be?
4 Why did the man take Aladdin to the cave?
5 Why couldn't Aladdin get out of the cave?
6 The genie says, 'Your wish is my command.' What does this mean?
7 The man gave Aladdin a ring. How was it useful?
8 Who was the man Aladdin had met in the street?

The story of Aladdin: Part 2

● What do you remember about the story of Aladdin so far?

Speaking

1 As a class, discuss the story so far.

1 Is it exciting?   *I think it's (exciting).*
2 Did anything surprise you?   *I was surprised that …*
3 Who is the most interesting character?
4 Which aspects of this story would make it good for a play or a film?

Use of English: *like* and *as* to say that things are similar

like

You're just *like* him. Aladdin ran *like* the wind.	In these sentences *like* means 'similar to' or 'the same as'.

as

As I told you, … NOT ~~Like~~ I told you. Do as I say. NOT Do ~~like~~ I say.	Use *as* (not *like*) before a subject + verb.

---

2 Complete the sentences with *like* or *as*.

1 Aladdin didn't want to be a tailor _____ his father.
2 The man came to Aladdin's house, _____ he had promised.
3 The man didn't look _____ Aladdin's father.
4 Aladdin did _____ the man told him and went into the cave.
5 'I will do _____ you wish,' said the genie to Aladdin.

Listening 33

3 Before you listen to the rest of the story, say what you think will happen.

4 Listen again. Match the two halves of each sentence to make a summary.

1 When Aladdin's mother rubbed the lamp,
2 Aladdin asked the Genie of the Lamp
3 One day, Aladdin saw the sultan's beautiful daughter, Badr-al-Budur, and
4 The sultan was so impressed by Aladdin's gifts of treasure that
5 The Genie of the Lamp provided a palace
6 The sorcerer travelled from Morocco to China
7 The sorcerer had some new lamps made and
8 A servant girl from the palace
9 The sorcerer used the magic lamp
10 The sultan gave Aladdin forty days
11 Aladdin asked the Genie of the Ring
12 The princess poisoned the sorcerer, and she and Aladdin

a fell in love with her.
b gave the sorcerer Aladdin's old lamp in exchange for a new one.
c for Aladdin and the princess to live in.
d to find the magic lamp.
e returned to China to live happily ever after.
f he allowed him to marry his daughter.
g the Genie of the Lamp appeared.
h to bring some food for him and his mother.
i to find his daughter.
j to take Aladdin's palace, the princess and himself to Morocco.
k to take him to the palace in Morocco.
l walked round the streets near the palace shouting, 'New lamps for old!'

Use of English: Reported speech – commands

Use *ask* or *tell* plus the *to* infinitive to report commands. Change the pronouns where necessary.

Direct command	Reported command
(Aladdin to the Genie of the Ring:) *'Take me to the palace in Morocco.'* →	Aladdin asked the Genie of the Ring to take him to the palace in Morocco.
(The sorcerer to Aladdin:) *'Give the gold coins to your mother.'* →	The sorcerer told Aladdin to give the gold coins to his mother.
(The sorcerer to Aladdin:) *'Don't lose the ring.'* →	The sorcerer told Aladdin not to lose the ring.

5 Report the commands.

(The sorcerer to Aladdin:)

1 'Lift the stone.'
   The sorcerer asked to Aladdin to lift the stone.
2 'Go down into the cave.'
3 'Give me the lamp.'

(Aladdin to the Genie of the Ring:)

4 *'Take me back home.'*

(Aladdin to the Genie of the Lamp:)

5 *'Bring us some good things to eat.'*
6 *'Take us all back to China.'*

(The sultan to Aladdin:)

7 *'Bring my daughter back to me.'*
8 *'Don't come back without her.'*

Project: Aladdin – the play

You are going to write and perform a play based on the story of Aladdin.

1 There are eight characters: Aladdin, Aladdin's mother, the sorcerer, the Genie of the Ring, the Genie of the Lamp, the sultan, the princess, the princess's servant.

2 There are six scenes in the play.

3 Work in six groups. Each group writes one scene from the play, using the script outline on the opposite page.

The dialogue for the start and the end of each scene is given in the outline. You need to write the dialogue for the rest of the scene. This is shown in *blue* in the outline. Look back at pages 144–147 to help you.

4 Your teacher will check your script.

5 You will need the following props:

an old lamp

some sand

a ring

some treasure

a new lamp

6 You are going to perform the scene you've written. Choose the parts you're going to play. If necessary, bring in students from other groups.

7 Rehearse your scene. Speak clearly and slowly and use movement and facial expressions to help the audience understand what you are saying. Your teacher will check your pronunciation.

8 Give a performance of *Aladdin*.

Aladdin

Describe where the scene takes place.

Scene 1 *China. Aladdin's house and the street outside.*

List the characters appearing in this scene.

ALADDIN, ALADDIN'S MOTHER, THE SORCERER

MOTHER: Aladdin! Where are you? You never help me in the house. You play with your friends all day …

ALADDIN: Bye, Mum! See you later!

Give stage directions.

Exit Aladdin.

[The sorcerer finds Aladdin, tells him he is his uncle, and promises him that he can become rich. But first Aladdin must help him …]

SORCERER: Come with me, Aladdin!

....

Scene 2 *China. In a beautiful garden.*

THE SORCERER, ALADDIN, THE GENIE OF THE RING

SORCERER: Now, Aladdin, you must lift this big stone and go into the cave.

[The sorcerer tells Aladdin what is in the cave: wonderful treasure … but also a lamp. He wants Aladdin to bring him the lamp. Aladdin is afraid, but the sorcerer gives Aladdin a ring to protect him. Aladdin goes into the cave, finds the treasure and the lamp, but he can't get out. The sorcerer gets angry and puts the stone back in front of the cave. Aladdin accidentally rubs the ring. The Genie of the Ring appears.]

GENIE OF THE RING: Your wish is my command! What do you want, Master?

ALADDIN: I want to get out of here!

....

Scene 3 *China. Aladdin's house.*

MOTHER, ALADDIN, THE GENIE OF THE LAMP

MOTHER: Aladdin! You're home at last! But where is your uncle?

[Aladdin explains that the man isn't his uncle, but a very bad man. Aladdin is hungry, but there's nothing to eat. His mother decides to clean the lamp, to sell it for some food. The Genie of the Lamp appears and brings food.]

MOTHER: This is wonderful!

Scene 4 *China. The market and the Sultan's palace.*

ALADDIN, MOTHER, THE GENIE OF THE LAMP, THE SULTAN, THE PRINCESS

ALADDIN: Mother, I've just seen the sultan's daughter. She is so beautiful. I'm in love with her. I want to marry her.

[Aladdin's mother explains that this is impossible: the Princess is rich, but they are poor. Aladdin says they can ask the Genie of the Lamp for money and jewels. He persuades his mother to take some treasure to the sultan.]

SULTAN: You may marry my daughter.

....

Scene 5 *China. Aladdin's palace.*

ALADDIN, THE PRINCESS, THE PRINCESS'S SERVANT, THE SORCERER, THE GENIE OF THE LAMP.

ALADDIN: You are my wife, we have a beautiful palace … we are so happy! And now I must go and see my dear mother.

PRINCESS: Give her my good wishes.

[Aladdin goes out. The sorcerer arrives at Aladdin's palace. 'New lamps for old,' he cries. The princess's servant gives him the magic lamp. The sorcerer makes the Genie of the Lamp appear.]

SORCERER: Take the princess, the palace and me to Morocco!

....

Scene 6 *Morocco. Aladdin's palace. China.*

THE PRINCESS, THE SORCERER, ALADDIN, THE GENIE OF THE RING, THE GENIE OF THE LAMP.

PRINCESS: Where am I?

[Suddenly, the princess and her palace are in Morocco! Meanwhile, in China, Aladdin comes home to find his palace has disappeared. He asks the Genie of the Ring to help him. The Genie takes Aladdin to Morocco. Aladdin gives the princess some poison to put in the sorcerer's drink. The sorcerer drinks the poison and dies. Aladdin appears. He asks the Genie of the Lamp to take him and the princess back to China.]

THE GENIES: And they all lived happily ever after!

The End

Review of Units 17–18
Vocabulary
Festivals

1 Fill in the missing words. Then choose either the verb or the noun to complete the sentences.

verbs	nouns
to sing	a song
to celebrate	a _____
to dance	a _____
to symbolise	a _____
to decorate	a _____

1 Some people say Russian blinis are *a symbol* of the sun.
2 At midnight on New Year's Eve, we sing a special _____ .
3 People _____ Chinese New Year in January or February.
4 The dragon _____ is one of the highlights of Chinese New Year celebrations.
5 During the festival of Diwali, people _____ their homes.

2 What are they? (They're all connected with festivals.)

1 Events that people organise in order to celebrate something.
festivities
2 They're all different colours and they light up the sky on special occasions.
3 A big fire that you make outside.
4 You put a candle in it and hang it up or carry it.
5 It's an imaginary animal; it's important in Chinese New Year festivities and it's made of paper, silk and wood.

At the theatre

3 Complete this account of a visit to the theatre with words from the box.

stage	orchestra	curtain	audience
costumes	actors	props	scenery

We went to the theatre on Saturday to see *Aladdin*. The *curtain*[1] went up to show a Chinese village. The _____[2] was quite simple: just some trees, a bridge and a river. But it was very good. You felt as though you were in China. There was a small _____[3] with some Chinese instruments, including a big drum.

In the opening scene, there were just two _____[4] on the _____[5], Aladdin and his mother. They were wearing lovely Chinese _____[6] in bright colours.

It was a really good performance. There weren't many _____[7], just the lamp, of course, and Aladdin's treasure, but the dialogue was so funny that it didn't matter. There were a lot of people in the _____[8] and everybody enjoyed the play.

Use of English

4 Complete the text with the correct prepositions: *in, on, at*.

The Moon Festival
The Chinese have celebrated the Moon Festival for over a thousand years.

It takes place *in*[1] autumn, _____[2] the end of September or the beginning of October. It is celebrated _____[3] the 15th day of the 8th month in the Chinese calendar, on the night of a full moon. The Moon Festival was made a Chinese public holiday _____[4] 2008.

5 Make compound adjectives using words from the two columns. Then use them in the sentences below.

horse	covered
home	drawn
brightly	lined
snow	made
fur	coloured

1 We had a ride in a *horse-drawn* sleigh.
2 The decorations were made of _____ paper.
3 My feet weren't cold because I was wearing _____ boots.
4 There were lots of delicious _____ dishes.
5 We saw _____ mountains from the plane.

6 Complete the sentences with *like* or *as*.

1 It's the first day of the school holidays. You can do *as* you want.
2 I'm _____ my sister. We're both quite tall and we've got dark hair.
3 I'm returning the book to you _____ I promised.
4 It was wonderful. It was _____ a dream come true.
5 He loves his food. He eats _____ a horse!

7 Report a teacher's commands:

1 'Learn your lines for the school play by Friday.'
(tell)   *The teacher told us to learn our lines for the school play by Friday.*
2 'Please come to the school hall at 4 o'clock.'
(ask)
3 'Don't be late for the rehearsal.'
(tell)
4 'Remember to bring your costumes.'
(tell)
5 'Don't touch the props or the scenery.'
(tell)
6 'Please practise your songs at home.'
(ask)

General knowledge quiz

8 Work with a partner. Answer the questions.

1 At Chinese New Year, what colour do people wear? What does it symbolise?
2 In Cuba at New Year, what do people eat at midnight?
3 When does the festival of Diwali take place and how long does it last?
4 What does the word 'diwali' mean?
5 When and where would you see a *rangoli* pattern?
6 When does Eid al-Fitr take place and how long does it last?
7 Does the festival of Eid begin when there is a new moon or a full moon?
8 When does Maslenitsa take place and where is it celebrated?
9 Who or what is Lady Maslenitsa, and what does she represent?
10 What are *blinis*?
11 When is April Fools' Day and what is it?
12 In 1957, why did British TV feature a family in Switzerland harvesting spaghetti from trees?
13 Where is the oldest known fun day celebrated? Is it Portugal, Iran or Sweden?
14 What do French and Italian children do on 1st April?
15 What do Portuguese children do on 1st April?
16 Where is Holi celebrated? And why is it sometimes called the 'festival of colours'?
17 What was Iran called in the past?
18 It has a fun day on 1st April and it's between Norway and Finland. Which country is it?
19 What is *The Thousand and One Nights*?
20 Name four of the main characters in *Aladdin*.

Acknowledgements

The authors and publishers would like to thank the following for their contribution to the development of Stage 7:

Series Editor: Peter Lucantoni; Development Editor: Sian Mavor; Project Manager: Charlotte al-Qadi; Reviewers: Liam Egan, MSc in TESOL; Lois Hopkins, MA Publishing; Ana Pérez Moreno, Licentiate in English Language and in Education; Claire Olmez, BEd, MA ELT; Mary Spratt; Graham Wilson.

Cover photo: ephotocorp/Alamy

The authors and publishers acknowledge the following sources of copyright material and are grateful for the permissions granted. While every effort has been made, it has not always been possible to identify the sources of all the material used, or to trace all copyright holders. If any omissions are brought to our notice, we will be happy to include the appropriate acknowledgements on reprinting.

p. 18 excerpt from *Hullabaloo in the Guava Orchard* by Kiran Desai, published by Faber and Faber, 1998; p. 34 'Postcard from School Camp' by Richard Caley was first published in *Bats, Balls and Balderdash* © Richard Caley, Durrington Press Ltd, used with permission of the author; p. 58 adapted from article 'Eating practices of the best endurance athletes in the world' by Owen Anderson Ph.D for Active.com; p. 67 from *War Horse* by Michael Morpurgo. Copyright © 1982 Michael Morpurgo. Published by Egmont UK Limited and used with permission. Reprinted by permission of Scholastic Inc.; p. 83 'To Give' by Vimal Shingadia, from the World Stories website, a collection of stories by children collected by Kids Out; p. 98 'Rain Falls Down' by Margot Henderson, used with permission from the author; p. 99 'Your Dresses' by Carol Ann Duffy, from *The Hat*, published by Faber and Faber Limited, 2007; p. 115 'In Daylight Strange' by Alan Brownjohn, copyright © Alan Brownjohn, 2009; p. 122 excerpts from *RACHEL'S DIARY* by Marissa Moss. Copyright © 1998 by Marissa Moss. Reprinted by permission of Houghton Mifflin Harcourt Publishing Company. All rights reserved; p. 127 adapted from 'A rainbow in silk' from *Stories from the Silk Road*, retold by Cherry Gilchrist, Barefoot Books, 1999; pp. 106-107 pen pal letter used by kind permission of Stormont House School, and Tina Yu letter used by kind permission of Tina Yu and Minsheng Junior High School, with thanks to Stormont House School.

Photo Acknowledgements

p.8: Superstock/UpperCut Images; p.9(header): Superstock/UpperCut Images; p.9 BL: Alamy/Robert Holmes; p.9 BR: Alamy/LOOK Die Bildagentur der Fotografen GmbH; p.11 (header): Superstock/UpperCut Images; p.12 a: Alamy/ITAR-TASS Photo Agency; p.13 (header): Superstock/UpperCut Images; p.12 b: Shutterstock/Hung Chung Chih; p.12 c: Corbis/Bettmann; p.12 d: Thinkstock/iStockphoto; p.14 T: Alamy/redsnapper; p.14 (Shamira): Shutterstock/Michael C. Gray; p.14 (Sunil): Shutterstock/Samuel Borges Photography; p.15(header): Alamy/redsnapper; p.16 TL: Alamy/Angela Hampton Picture Library; p.16 TC: Alamy/Oote Boe; p.16 TR: Thinkstock/Stockbyte; p.16 C: Shutterstock/ZouZou; p.16 B: Thinkstock/DigitalVision; p.17 (header): Alamy/redsnapper; p.19 (header): Alamy/redsnapper; p.19: Art Directors & Trip/Helene Rogers; p.21 (header): Alamy/redsnapper; p.23: Alamy/ITAR-TASS Photo Agency; p.23 (header): Alamy/redsnapper; p.24: Corbis/KidStock/Blend Images; p.25 (header): Corbis/KidStock/Blend Images; p.27 (header): Corbis/KidStock/Blend Images; p.28 a: Alamy/Lenscap; p.28 b: Art Directors & Trip/Helene Rogers; p.28 c: GTX Corp GPS Smart Shoe; p.28 d: Michelle Poole, The Design Poole; p.28 e: Press Association Images/Jae C. Hong/AP; p.28 f: Press Association Images/Ron Harris/AP; p.29 (header): Corbis/KidStock/Blend Images; p.29: "BUFF® and the ways to wear icons are registered trademark properties of Original BUFF SA"; p.30 T: Thinkstock/iStockphoto; p.30 C: Alamy/StockShot; p.30 B: Shutterstock/Chris Turner; p.31 (header): Thinkstock/iStockphoto; p.32 B: Alamy/David Wall; p.33 (header): Thinkstock/iStockphoto; p.33: Alamy/Nik Taylor Sport; p.34 T: Shutterstock/fotum; p.34 C: Thinkstock/iStockphoto; p.34 B: Alamy/Martin Shields; p.35 (header): Thinkstock/iStockphoto; p.37 (header): Thinkstock/iStockphoto; p.39 (header): Thinkstock/iStockphoto; p.40 T: Alamy/Chris Hellier; p.40 BR: Shutterstock/Imagefoto55; p.40 BL: Alamy/Distinctive Images; p.40 a: Shutterstock/cowardlion; p.40 b: Alamy/Pep Roig; p.40 c: Alamy/Marion Kaplan; p.40 d: Shutterstock/Pavel L Photo and Video; p.40 e: Alamy/Mo Peerbacus; p.41 (header): Alamy/Chris Hellier; p.42 3: Alamy/David Thorpe; p.42 5: Corbis/Bettmann; p.42 1: Shutterstock/wen mingming; p.42 6: Alamy/Heritage Image Partnership Ltd; p.43 (header): Alamy/Chris Hellier; p.45 (header): Alamy/Chris Hellier; p.46: Thinkstock/iStockphoto; p.47 (header): Thinkstock/iStockphoto; p.49 (header): Thinkstock/iStockphoto; p.50: Thinkstock/Jupiterimages; p.51 (header): Thinkstock/iStockphoto; p.53 (header): Thinkstock/iStockphoto; p.54: Shutterstock/Gabi Siebenhuehner; p.55 (header): Thinkstock/iStockphoto; p.56: Science Photo Library/Maximilian Stock Ltd; p.57 (header): Science Photo Library/Maximilian Stock Ltd; p.59 (header): Science Photo Library/Maximilian Stock Ltd; p.59: Thinkstock/iStockphoto/Xiangdong Li; p.60: Alamy/John Warburton-Lee Photography; p.61 (header): Science Photo Library/Maximilian Stock Ltd; p.62 a: Shutterstock/Gucio_55; p.62 b: Thinkstock/iStockphoto/Cathy Keifer; p.62 c: Thinkstock/iStockphoto; p.62 d: Shutterstock/bluehand; p.62 e: Shutterstock/Nacho Such; p.63 (header): Shutterstock/Gucio_55;

p.64 R: Thinkstock/iStockphoto; p.64 L: Shutterstock/Monkey Business Images; p.65 (header): Shutterstock/Gucio_55; p.66: Thinkstock/iStockphoto; p.67 (header): Shutterstock/Gucio_55; p.67: Thinkstock/iStockphoto/Dezhi Wei; p.68: Rex Features/Donald Cooper; p.71 (header): Shutterstock/Gucio_55; p.71: Thinkstock/iStockphoto/Cathy Keifer; p.72: Getty Images/Julian Finney; p.73 (header): Getty Images/Julian Finney; p.74: Getty Images/Julian Finney; p.75 (header): Getty Images/Julian Finney; p.76: Alamy/Viktor Cap; p.77 (header): Getty Images/Julian Finney; p.77 L: Thinkstock/Purestock; p.78: Thinkstock/Goodshoot; p.79 (header): Thinkstock/Goodshoot; p.79: Alamy/SNS Group; p.80T: Shutterstock/Dan Breckwoldt; p.80 B: Thinkstock/AbleStock.com; p.81 (header): Thinkstock/Goodshoot; p.82 (boy soccer): Thinkstock/Comstock; p.82 (earth): Thinkstock/iStockphoto; p.82 (apple): Thinkstock/iStockphoto; p.82 (laptop): Thinkstock/iStockphoto; p.83 (header): Thinkstock/Goodshoot; p.84: Mary Evans Picture Library p.85 (header): Thinkstock/Goodshoot; p.87: Thinkstock/Goodshoot; p.88 T: Thinkstock/iStockphoto; p.88 B: Thinkstock/iStockphoto; p.89 (header): Thinkstock/iStockphoto; p.91 (header): Thinkstock/iStockphoto; p.92: Alamy/Mitch Diamond; p.93: Thinkstock/iStockphoto; p.94: Thinkstock/Photodisc; p.95 (header): Thinkstock/Photodisc; p.97 (header): Thinkstock/Photodisc; p.97: Thinkstock/Hemera; p.98: Getty Images/Bloomberg; p.99 (header): Thinkstock/Photodisc; p.99: Rex Features/View Pictures; p.101 (header): Thinkstock/Photodisc; p.101 TL: Thinkstock/iStockphoto; p.101 TR: Thinkstock/Ingram Publishing; p.101 B: Thinkstock/iStockphoto; p.103 (header): Thinkstock/Photodisc; p.104: Alamy/David Grossman; p.105(header): Shutterstock/Monkey Business Images; p.105: Shutterstock/Zurijeta; p.106: La Cecilia; p.107 (header): Alamy/David Grossman; p.108: Corbis/David Madison; p.109 (header): Alamy/David Grossman; p.109: photos from Tina Yu used with permission, with thanks to Tina, her family and Minsheng Junior High School, Taipei; p.110: Alamy/JLImages; p.111 (header): Alamy/JLImages; p.112 T: Shutterstock/Kevin Eaves; p.112 B: Thinkstock/iStockphoto; p.113 (header): Alamy/JLImages; p.115 (header): Alamy/JLImages; p.115: ACTED; p.117 (header): Alamy/JLImages; p.119 (header): Alamy/JLImages; p.119: Shutterstock p.120B: Alamy/ North Wind Picture Archives; p.120 T: Corbis/John C.H. Grabill; p.121 (header): Corbis/John C.H. Grabill; p.122: Corbis/John C.H. Grabill; p.123 (header): Corbis/John C.H. Grabill; p.125 (header): Corbis/John C.H. Grabill; p.125 American Pioneer Family, c.1870 (b/w photo), American Photographer, (19th century) / Private Collection / Peter Newark American Pictures / The Bridgeman Art Library; p.126: Thinkstock/Zoonar; p.127 (header): Thinkstock/Zoonar; p.129 (header): Thinkstock/Zoonar; p.131 (header): Thinkstock/Zoonar; p.133 (header): Thinkstock/Zoonar; p.135 (header): Thinkstock/Zoonar; p.136: Thinkstock/iStockphoto; p.137 (header): Thinkstock/iStockphoto; p.137: Shutterstock/Jose Gil; p.138 L: Alamy/Tim Gainey; p.138 R: Corbis/Hemant Mehta /India Picture; p.139 (header): Thinkstock/iStockphoto; p.139 L: Shutterstock/highviews; p.141 (header): Thinkstock/iStockphoto; p.139 R: Alamy/Image Asset Management Ltd; p.140: Copyright©BBC Photo Library; p.141: Alamy/epa european pressphoto agency b.v.; p.142: Thinkstock/iStockphoto; p.144: Public Domain; p.145 (header): Thinkstock/iStockphoto; p.146: Alamy/ Lebrecht Music and Arts Photo Library; p.147 (header): Thinkstock/iStockphoto; p.149 (header): Thinkstock/iStockphoto; p.151 (header): Thinkstock/iStockphoto.

Illustrations

David Banks pp 16, 36, 37, 111, 114, 142; Dylan Gibson pp 29, 45, 53, 69, 129; David Russell pp 18, 30, 44 (left), 46, 47, 48 (top), 79, 80, 90, 94, 95, 96, 102; David Shephard (Bright Agency) pp 21, 26, 39, 51, 73, 84, 116–117, 124; Norbert Sipos (Beehive Illustration) pp 77, 100, 110, 119, 126–127, 132, 133; Mark Turner (Beehive Illustration) pp 10, 24, 32, 42, 44 (right), 48 (bottom), 14.

Development of this publication has made use of the Cambridge English Corpus (CEC). The CEC is a multi-billion word computer database of contemporary spoken and written English. It includes British English, American English and other varieties of English. It also includes the Cambridge Learner Corpus, developed in collaboration with Cambridge English Language Assessment. Cambridge University Press has built up the CEC to provide evidence about language use that helps to produce better language teaching materials.

This product is informed by the English Vocabulary Profile, built as part of the English Profile, a collaborative programme designed to enhance the learning, teaching and assessment of English worldwide. Its main funding partners are Cambridge University Press and Cambridge English Language Assessment and its aim is to create a 'profile' for English linked to the Common European Framework of Reference for Languages (CEFR). English Profile outcomes, such as the English Vocabulary Profile, will provide detailed information about the language that learners can be expected to demonstrate at each CEFR level, offering a clear benchmark for learners' proficiency. For more information, please visit www.englishprofile.org.